THE
EUCHARISTIC PRAYER
AT SUNDAY MASS

Richard McCarron

LTP

LITURGY
TRAINING
PUBLICATIONS

ACKNOWLEDGMENTS

Thanks be first to God, who directs all works from beginning to end through the Holy Spirit! Thanks be to God for my friends, who through thick and very thin have supported and encouraged this undertaking: questioning, reading and conversing on any number of matters of table fellowship. Thanks be to God for Gabe Huck, a sagacious and masterful editor, who had the courage and confidence to charge me with this tome; for J-Glenn Murray, SJ, a true and mighty friend, who convinced me I should take on the project and without whose support I would never have made it through; for John Francis Baldovin, SJ, Catherine Dooley, OP, Mark Francis, CSV, Jerome Hall, SJ, Sabrina Marie Kersanac and George Philip Miller, whose comments on drafts of the manuscript were invaluable. Thanks be, too, for the number of assemblies whose eucharistic praying animates the words here printed, and for my parents and grandparents, those still here and those feasting now with the Lamb, through whom I truly know the steadfast love of God.

Richard Edward McCarron
v. domenica per annum MCMXCVII

This book was edited by Gabe Huck. Deborah Bogaert was the production editor, with assistance from Theresa Houston. It was designed by M. Urgo and typeset in Trump Mediaeval and Tiepolo by Phyllis Martinez. The photos on pages 11, 69 and 105 are by Eileen Crowley-Horak. The photos on pages 39, 93 and 131 are by Antonio Pérez. The photo on page 121 is by Regina Kuehn. Printed by Bawden Printing of Eldridge, Iowa.

ISBN 1-56854-021-3
EPSUN

Cover: A sixteenth-century icon from central Ethiopia, tempera on gesso-covered wood panels. The paschal mystery proclaimed and affirmed in the eucharistic prayer is seen here in a triptych where ancient images tell again the passion, death and resurrection of the Lord. The glorious cross is central and its eucharistic presence is seen in the blood of Christ poured out and taken in chalices by angels. The cross is surrounded by scenes of the interrogation and torture, of the deposition and burial. The upper panel on the left shows the descent into hell, the ancient image of resurrection: Christ, who in dying has conquered death, grasps the hands of Adam and Eve in an image that seems to mirror baptism. Photo by Malcolm Varon, © 1993.

CONTENTS

CAN THESE BONES LIVE?

Down in the valley, God asked the prophet Ezekiel a mighty question: "Mortal, can these dry bones live?" (Ezekiel 37:3). Today, this question is being posed once more to those who are charged with the preparation and celebration of the Sunday liturgy — the assembly that celebrates, the ministers from within that assembly who prepare and serve, and those ordained as priests or bishops who preside.

We have come a long way since the early days of the conciliar reform of the liturgy: Assemblies respond and sing, the word is proclaimed with dignity and reverence, careful attention is given to environment and season, and all come to the communion table. Many assemblies strive to realize fully week after week the vision of the Council: that the eucharistic liturgy be seen, heard, felt and smelt as the "summit toward which the activity of the church is directed . . . the source from which all its power flows."[1] This is critical work if we are utterly convinced that "the preeminent manifestation of the church is present in the full, active participation of all God's holy people in these liturgical celebrations" (SC, 41).

But many still know liturgical assemblies that are but shadows of who they are called to be and celebrations that are slivers of what they could be. Many stand at the brink of the valley and behold dry bones. And when we come to the eucharistic prayer, named the central prayer of the Sunday liturgy, we behold very dry bones indeed. The question is put forth: Can these dry bones live?

We have come to realize that liturgy is something people do, something people live. The eucharistic prayer is more than its words: It is a way of praying and living. What lies in the ritual book must be enfleshed when we gather. We come together and breathe life into our rituals and their words. We can do this because we have first been sealed in the Spirit, the one who aids us in our weakness to pray "that very Spirit intercedes with sighs too deep for words" (Romans 8:26).

WHAT'S THE DIFFERENCE?

The *General Instruction of the Roman Missal* boldly states, "The center and summit of the entire celebration begins: the eucharistic prayer, a prayer of thanksgiving and sanctification. . . . The entire congregation joins itself to Christ in acknowledging the great things God has done" (54).

Yet more often than not, the eucharistic prayer is still perceived as something that the priest alone does. What is there to change that perception, to manifest that the eucharistic prayer is the prayer of the whole people of God gathered? We still take for granted medieval practice and piety. They haunt our attempts to live up to the call of the Council. The centuries-old notion that the eucharistic prayer is something that the clergy do while the people look on is difficult to undo, even when the assembly has appropriated its role in other parts of the Sunday liturgy. As a result, we experience other moments of the liturgy as more involving of the assembly and thus as more central: the Gloria, the Sign of Peace, the Lord's Prayer.

But few assemblies claim the eucharistic prayer as their own. "It is rarely a lived moment of participation by the assembly 'making eucharist together.'"[2] Are we not embarrassed to find a central prayer whose words often are spoken inattentively — and heard just as inattentively? Are we not ashamed to realize that our acclamations are little more than a peep when they are meant to shake earth and heaven? We need desperately to discover the dynamics of the great thanksgiving prayer. For the first time in over a thousand years in our Roman Catholic church, the entire eucharistic prayer is being prayed aloud. What difference has it made? What difference can it make if an assembly regularly joins to make this prayer central?

Here is a bold answer: The difference that grasping the dynamic of the eucharistic prayer, praying it well and embodying it at Sunday Mass can make (as we shall see) is the difference between life and death. The living out of our baptismal life as daughters and sons of God is at stake.

EUCHARISTIC PRAYING: THEN, NOW AND TO COME

This volume intends to show what eucharistic praying entails and how it could be done every Sunday. Because so much is involved in present practice and because the stakes are so high, this effort demands much study, reflection and discussion.

The Church Constituting Itself

We forget who we are, where we came from, where we are headed. So we assemble when it is timely, to invest ourselves as a community of Christians in liturgical anamnesis. The self-engaging activity of our liturgy not only causes us to remember who we are; it invites us to commit ourselves to a life congruent with our identity.

All liturgy is anamnesis. Sunday eucharist is the center of Christian anamnesis. This is the weekly occasion on which the baptized assemble to reconstitute themselves publicly in their identity as the church of Jesus Christ. The church is reconstituting itself publicly, attempting to put on the mind of Christ when it celebrates the liturgy of the word. The church is reconstituting itself as a priestly people when it prays the prayer of general intercession.

But the church acts most profoundly in the Sunday assembly to reconstitute itself as the Body of Christ. In Sunday eucharistic liturgy we move through public praise and thanksgiving for the mystery; we remember, and remembering dare to move even nearer to our shared identification in the mystery of Christ. Through sacramental communion in the body broken for the world's life and the blood poured out for the world's forgiveness, each of us engages ourselves, each of us commits ourselves, and the church is reconstituted by God's gift to us.

Our constitution as church is always partial, never exhaustive. So we must reassemble every Lord's Day. We are burdened by the limit of our comprehension of inexhaustible mystery. We are also limited by the inauthenticity which comes from having divided identities, dual commitments to serve our own purposes as well as God's.

Excerpts from Mary Collins, Contemplative Participation: Sacrosanctum Concilium *Twenty-five Years Later. (Collegeville: Liturgical Press, 1990), pp. 54–57. © 1990 Liturgical Press. Used with permission.*

Our work in this volume begins in realizing what thanksgiving and memory mean and in situating them as the basis for Christian eucharistic prayer. To speak about the eucharistic prayer today means also that we need to survey its history — why things are the way they are today. To this end, we will briefly explore how the eucharistic prayer was shaped, how it grew and how it has been understood and misunderstood throughout the history of the church. To recover the eucharistic prayer

Mystery of Faith

In order that the eucharistic mystery be celebrated as the "mystery of faith," it is necessary that this be done in as effective as possible an act of faith by the Church in all [the] members. Hence the importance of a eucharistic prayer in which this living faith which receives the mystery is expressed fully, directly and comprehensibly. . . . As the Jews already understood, the liturgical *berakoth* in their totality take on their full sense only if they extend into the whole life of the pious Jew or the faithful Christian through a constantly renewed attitude of eucharistic prayer and sacrifice. Indeed, it is our whole life and all things with us that are to be consecrated through the eucharist to the glory of God, in Christ, by the power of the Spirit.

The ideal eucharist does not have one form in tradition, but rather complementary forms which illuminate one another. . . . The complete eucharist is always a confession of God as creator and redeemer, through Christ, and more especially a glorification of God enlightening us with knowledge, vivifying us with [God's] own life, in the supreme gift of

[God's] own Spirit. At the same time, and inseparably, this eucharist is a supplication that the mystery being celebrated have its complete fulfilment in us, in the perfect church and all the members. It concludes with the representation to God of the memorial of this sacred mystery, together with the invocation that [God] consecrated our union with the sacrifice of [the] Son and bring it to its eschatological perfection through the power of the Spirit. Thus in concert, as one in *the* One, we shall eternally glorify the Father together with the angelic powers. This . . . invocation gathers all of our . . . supplications for the growth of the Church as the body of Christ and for the salvation of the world, and crowns the supplication that summed them all up: that the Father, in the memorial of [the] Son, accept all the prayers and all the sacrifices that this . . . People present, by making them one . . . prayer and one sacrifice, Christ's own eucharist and [Christ's] own cross.

Excerpts from Louis Bouyer, Eucharist: The Theology and Spirituality of the Eucharistic Prayer *(Notre Dame: University of Notre Dame Press, 1968), pp. 470–471. © 1968 University of Notre Dame Press. Used with permission.*

requires that we unfold what is set out in the sacramentary and in the ten prayers of the Roman Rite.

Then we can set out what the work of the assembly and the role of the presider entail and look forward to what might come. That which might come to be will require careful catechesis and strong preaching. To stimulate the imagination and engage both mind and heart, the narrative of this volume is often homiletic in style. Here, preachers and teachers can find a resource for their work. The medium here intends to be as helpful as the message. Homilists and teachers should take what they can from the writing and images of this book as they preach and teach toward full participation in the eucharistic prayer.

While the most practical guidance for liturgy teams, musicians, the assembly and presiders comes in the latter chapters, this guidance is grounded in the earlier chapters. Good posture, effective ritual strategies, wise choice of texts and powerful use of music follow upon realizing that the eucharistic prayer is part and parcel of the vocation of all the baptized and flows from living lives of thanksgiving and praise.

Those who are responsible for parish liturgy will find guidance for beginning their work of fostering the full celebration of the eucharistic prayer. And for those who find their parish's celebration of the eucharistic prayer adequate, this book offers criteria for evaluating practice and offers directions for refining liturgical celebration. Above all else, the concrete situation of the parish needs to become the reader's reflections in the margins. Then, from the foundations and vision set out in the pages that follow, each parish can engage in the crucial work of embodying the eucharistic prayer in its own local context: the shape and design of the worship space, the resources of ministers and music, and above all, the local culture.

While this book focuses on the eucharistic prayer, we need to remember always that the eucharistic prayer is integrally bound to the whole celebration of the liturgy, from gathering to dismissal. While the eucharistic prayer is the climax of the liturgy, it is ordered to the communion table where we feast on the Body and Blood of Christ.[3] So what is said about the eucharistic prayer must not be isolated from the the whole liturgical celebration.

Ezekiel stood amazed as bones came together, bound by sinew and covered with flesh. As the breath came into them, the multitude lived. Thus was he able to promise life and land to the withered house of Israel (Ezekiel 37:8–14). So, too, we might stand amazed as we gather about the altar-table, name the mighty and merciful things God has done for us in Christ Jesus, and call upon the Spirit to come. Praying the eucharistic prayer well transforms our lives and molds our vision in such a way that we witness God's action here and now and taste and see how good God is in our communion. For that we do sing with every fiber of our being: Amen!

NOTES

1. *The Constitution on the Sacred Liturgy, Sacrosanctum Concilium* (hereafter SC), in *Vatican Council II: Constitutions, Decrees, Declarations*, ed. Austin Flannery (New York: Costello Publishing, 1996): # 10.

2. Joseph Gelineau, *The Eucharistic Prayer: Praise of the Whole Assembly* (Washington, D.C.: Pastoral Press, 1985), 1.

3. For an insightful vision of what the communion rite can be, see Gabe Huck, *The Communion Rite at Sunday Mass* (Chicago: Liturgy Training Publications, 1989).

THE ROOTS AND EVOLUTION OF EUCHARISTIC PRAYING

ur eucharistic praying calls us back to our roots, back to an ancient time and distant place where the psalmist stands with lyre in hand. We Christians have inherited from our Jewish forebears a way of praying and a way of being. The fundamental dimensions of our prayer and our life are praise, thanksgiving and supplication. A return to these roots can help us grasp what is at stake today in Christian eucharistic praying.

Central to our forebears' lives was this faith: We are a people bound up in covenant with God.

> I will establish my covenant between me and you,
> and your offspring after you throughout their generations,
> for an everlasting covenant,
> to be God to you and to your offspring after you. Genesis 17:7

This God who makes such a covenant is a God of blessing: ordering chaos, arraying the earth and sky, fashioning humankind in the divine image, bringing life from barrenness and bringing fruitfulness from flood. And God, the God of Abraham and Sarah and their descendants, acts in steadfast love and faithfulness. God has embraced humankind and directed our path toward life. We would be counted as naught were it not for God's blessing and covenant with us:

> What is humankind
> that you remember them,
> the human race

that you care for them?
You treat them like gods,
dressing them in glory and splendor. Psalm 8:5–6

Dressed in glory and honor, we know that the power and blessing of God undergird all we have and do. We realize that God rouses us from slumber, gives us the very breath we draw and the light that illumines the day, clothes us and provides the food and drink we share.

What gift can ever repay God's gift to me? asks the psalmist (Psalm 116:12). Only words of thanks and praise, given voice by breath that is itself gift. Every moment of our daily lives occasions thanks and praise to God. We acknowledge God as blessed, and all of life and the world as blessed because it is from God, who has entered into relationship with us.[1]

Throughout the First Testament, God lives in lasting relationship with the covenant people. God can be counted on to act on their behalf. And the wonderful works of God to humankind are mighty indeed! In the midst of slavery under Pharaoh, God cries freedom. In the pangs of hunger and desperation of thirst in the parched desert, God provides. Over the clamor of strange gods and through the gleam of golden calves, God binds all ever more deeply in the covenant of the Law. In the throes of destruction and desolation, God creates anew and leads people home. And in spite of failure and infidelity, God stretches out a hand and calls once more to the beloved. And Israel responds:

What god compares with you?
Who is like you, Lord of might,
clothed in truth, a God of power? Psalm 89:7, 9

Miriam surely knew no other god that could compare. She, delivered from bondage by God's outstretched arm and mighty hand, took a tambourine in hand and danced her praise and thanksgiving. What else could she do, standing dry-shod in safety? She danced and sang of God's steadfast love:

I sing of the Lord,
great and triumphant:

The Roots and Evolution of Eucharistic Praying

horse and rider
are cast into the sea! Exodus 15:21

Miriam's song of thanksgiving is not only on her lips but is given shape in her dance and beauty in the tambourine's music. Her body sways and her feet rhythmically sound upon the earth to proclaim how steadfast is her God.

Israel comes to know that the God who acts in such mighty ways for the whole assembly will act also for the household and the individual. God persists in love, maintains the promise of blessing and delivers the one who is sick, imprisoned, under siege, lost at sea, grieving, starving, dying. The helpless one calls out to God, and God hears the cry. God's response elicits praise and thanksgiving from the one delivered. Once more, the psalmist tells the story:

> They wandered through wasteland,
> trekked over sands,
> finding no city, no home.
> Weak from hunger and thirst,
> their lives were fading away.
> Then they cried out to God,
> who snatched them from danger.
> Let them celebrate God's love. Psalm 107:4–6, 8

This celebration of God's love, this thanks and praise, becomes an act of worship. In Psalm 116 the psalmist sings,

> The Lord hears me;
> the Lord bends to my voice
> whenever I call.
> Death had me in its grip. . . .
> I cried out for God. Psalm 116:2–4

The psalmist now rests secure in God's arms and vows to praise God, to report to others the steadfast love of God and to give thanks and praise in the assembly. In a sense, the delivered one gives testimony to the saving act of God, evoking from others the same praise and thanksgiving for the power of God. "Testimony before others of the wonderful deed of God to deliver the sufferer or the afflicted is at the heart of the thanksgiving prayer."[2] The testimony of the delivered one affirms for the assembly (and those beyond it who hear) the raucous praise: God has done it again! And there is perhaps no more valid testimony than that which is given by those who had good reason to distrust.

Time and again, to the burdened, the mourning, the lowly, God comes. And truly they give thanks. Their thanks, though, are not isolated, hollow thank-yous on the lips of those free to go their way.

> Even as songs of thanksgiving recount the story of the plight
> of the one delivered, the subject matter is not really the
> individual but the help of God. The hymns of praise simply
> expand that movement outward, away from the human
> creature and the community toward God.[3]

God is at the center, God is the one who has acted, God has delivered, God is praised. But that circle of praise grows ever wider:

> I will proclaim your name to my people,
> I will praise you in the assembly. . . .
> I will sing of you in the great assembly. . . .
> All races will bow to the Lord. . . .
> all destined to die bow low. . . .
> My children will serve,
> will proclaim God to the future,
> announcing to peoples yet unborn,
> "God saves." Psalm 22:23, 26, 28, 30–32

Thanksgiving "is not a private act. It arises out of relationship and further enhances and strengthens it."[4]

Not only is the act of thanksgiving itself worship, but it is bolstered by ritual gesture. The psalmist speaks of bringing "a gift of thanks" and raising the "cup of freedom as I call on God's name" (Psalm 116:13). Words of praise and thanksgiving are integrated with ritual gestures so that the whole of praise and thanks is embodied by the worshipers.

The mighty deeds of God's steadfast love, the unwavering call to God in need, and the merciful response of God elicits praise and thanksgiving. And God is not only the Mighty One who tramples the Egyptians and delivers the people to freedom—God is also the God of the

The mighty deeds of God's steadfast love, the unwavering call to God in need, and the merciful response of God elicit praise and thanksgiving.

weak, the poor and the afflicted. Both are plainly the action of God writ large and small.

> It is no accident, therefore, that when the people sang their hymns of praise and songs of thanksgiving, they praised God for showing, both in all cases and in their particular case, that the claim is true, that the steadfast love of God could be counted on and that God's way . . . is truly merciful and gracious.[5]

But there were many times when it seemed that God had indeed forgotten what was promised. And likewise, there were many times when the people forgot that God alone was to be their God. The prophets realized that when God was abandoned or the people felt abandoned in the face of impending disaster, they had to take radical action. What could the prophets do when God was nowhere to be found and every divine promise seemingly lay in ruins? Just this: Echo the voice of God to chaos, ring out the solemn promise to Abraham, summon the voice of Miriam on the shore and dance!

In the midst of loss, sin and destruction, the prophet discerns the ways that God has acted in fidelity. Through the language of praise and thanksgiving, the way of speaking graven on the beloved of God, the prophet puts God right "at the center of a scene from which we presumed God had fled."[6] The prophet, starting with the situation of the people, mines their memory for the astonishing ways in which God has acted in steadfast love and faithfulness in the past. To the present situation of hopelessness, the prophet lets the world know that God keeps promises, that God acts, and the state of affairs will not remain the same. The people proclaim that God acts in power and love, and so the world is transformed.[7] Made confident and restored with hope that in God new things are possible, the people plead with God to act once more on their behalf.

The priest and scribe Ezra engages this prophetic outlook and brings it to public expression in a great prayer of praise and thanksgiving. After the initial blessing of God, Ezra praises God in the midst of the assembly, calling up pivotal moments of God's saving action: creation from naught, the call of Abraham, the Exodus, the giving of the Law, the sustenance in the desert, the establishment of kingdoms, the possession of the land, the sending of the prophets.

Ezra confesses, too, that the people had strayed, sinned and abandoned God. Yet even in the most desperate of situations, they cried out, and God answered them in ways beyond their expectations. God is gracious, steadfast in love and faithful to the promise never to forget. And God's people are created, called, liberated and loved. As Ezra speaks, God's order, God's rule, God's way of looking at things is opened up here and now. Who could ever have thought that a nobody would father the generations, a barren woman give birth, a trampled people dance for freedom, a sinful folk be embraced time and again? But God spoke, and it came to pass, writ large and writ small.

The hope and promise Ezra names in each of the events energizes the people. It shapes the way the world is supposed to be; it names God as the Holy One of Israel; it engages God's merciful love, demonstrated to have no bounds. The hope that wells up from the promise bursts out in a call to God to act once more. And so Ezra can then boldly plead:

"Now therefore, our God—the great and mighty and awesome God, keeping covenant and steadfast love—do not treat lightly all the hardship that has come upon us" (Nehemiah 9:32). Ezra invokes God to act once more here and now to forgive transgression and to remember the covenant, knowing full well that the future will not look the same.

To Keep Memorial

Here we cut to the heart of what it means to remember.[8] Ezra names the outstanding moments of God's saving intervention. In prayer before God and in the midst of the assembly, Ezra reminds both God and the people of the irrevocable covenant relationship that has been forged between them. As he prays, their identity as the covenanted people of God is asserted. As he prays, this identity is thrust in the face of the powers that be and challenges the world of despair and anxiety.

As Ezra names the call of Abraham, the exodus from Egypt, the giving of the Law and the beckon of the prophets, the people are not transported to some faraway age. Nor is some faraway age enfleshed before them, as if they were rushing through the parted sea or were being sated with manna. Rather, the naming of these foundational events bespeaks the living relationship the people has with God, who always acts in decisive ways in their history. The very remembering of the mighty deeds of God disrupts the way things are *now* as much as the events named turned their ancestors' world on end *then*.[9] The very remembering undoes the powers that be and trounces the thought that what is, is all there is.

To remember is to proclaim who this people really is and what this people will be. These people are who they are today because of what God has done. They can live today and rise tomorrow because of their past.[10] To remember is not to plunge ourselves back into the good old days, to long for the way things used to be. The past is passed. But we are who we are today because the past makes today possible. And we will not be the same tomorrow, because we know from our past that God remembers who we are.

Above All Blessing and Praise

The Levites, Jeshua, Kadmiel, Bani, Hashab-neiah, Sherebiah, Hodiah, Shebaniah, and Pethahiah, said, "Stand up and bless the LORD your God from everlasting to everlasting. Blessed be your glorious name, which is exalted above all blessing and praise."

And Ezra said: "You are the LORD, you alone; you have made heaven, the heaven of heavens, with all their host, the earth and all that is on it, the seas and all that is in them. To all of them you give life, and the host of heaven worships you. You are the LORD, the God who chose Abram and brought him out of Ur of the Chaldeans and gave him the name Abraham; and you found his heart faithful before you, and made with him a covenant to give to his descendants the land of the Canaanite, the Hittite, the Amorite, the Perizzite, the Jebusite, and the Girgashite; and you have fulfilled your promise, for you are righteous.

"And you saw the distress of our ancestors in Egypt and heard their cry at the Red Sea. You performed signs and wonders against Pharaoh and all his servants and all the people of his land, for you knew that they acted insolently against our ancestors. You made a name for yourself, which remains to this day. And you divided the sea before them, so that they passed through the sea on dry land, but you threw their pursuers into the depths, like a stone into mighty waters.

Moreover, you led them by day with a pillar of cloud, and by night with a pillar of fire, to give them light on the way in which they should go. You came down also upon Mount Sinai, and spoke with them from heaven, and gave them right ordinances and true laws, good statutes and commandments, and you made known your holy sabbath to them and gave them commandments and statutes and a law through your servant Moses. For their hunger you gave them bread from heaven, and for their thirst you brought water for them out of the rock, and you told them to go in to possess the land that you swore to give them.

"But they and our ancestors acted presumptuously and stiffened their necks and did not obey your commandments; they refused to obey, and were not mindful of the wonders that you performed among them; but they stiffened their necks and determined to return to their slavery in Egypt.

"But you are a God ready to forgive, gracious and merciful, slow to anger and abounding in steadfast love, and you did not forsake them. Even when they had cast an image of a calf for themselves and said, 'This is your God who brought you up out of Egypt,' and had committed great blasphemies, you in your great mercies did not forsake them in the wilderness; the pillar of cloud that led them in the way did not leave them by day, nor the pillar of fire by night that gave them light on the way by which they should go. You gave your good spirit to instruct them, and did not withhold your manna from their mouths, and gave them water for their thirst.

Forty years you sustained them in the wilderness so that they lacked nothing; their clothes did not wear out and their feet did not swell. And you gave them kingdoms and peoples, and allotted to them every corner, so they took possession of the land of King Sihon of Heshbon and the land of King Og of Bashan. You multiplied their descendants like the stars of heaven, and brought them into the land that you had told their ancestors to enter and possess.

"So the descendants went in and possessed the land, and you subdued before them the inhabitants of the land, the Canaanites, and gave them into their hands, with their kings and the peoples of the land, to do with them as they pleased. And they captured fortress cities and a rich land, and took possession of houses filled with all sorts of goods, hewn cisterns, vineyards, olive orchards, and fruit trees in abundance; so they ate, and were filled and became fat, and delighted themselves in your great goodness.

"Nevertheless they were disobedient and rebelled against you and cast your law behind their backs and killed your prophets, who had warned them in order to turn them back to you, and they committed great blasphemies. Therefore you gave them into the hands of their enemies, who made them suffer. Then in the time of their suffering they cried out to you and you heard them from heaven, and according to your great mercies you gave them saviors who saved them from the hands of their enemies. But after they had rest, they again did evil before you, and you abandoned them to the hands of their enemies, so that they had dominion over them;

"Yet when they turned and cried to you, you heard from heaven, and many times you rescued them according to your mercies. And you warned them in order to turn them back to your law. Yet they acted presumptuously and did not obey your commandments, but sinned against

your ordinances, by the observance of which a person shall live. They turned a stubborn shoulder and stiffened their neck and would not obey. Many years you were patient with them, and warned them by your spirit through your prophets; yet they would not listen. Therefore you handed them over to the peoples of the lands. Nevertheless, in your great mercies you did not make an end of them or forsake them, for you are a gracious and merciful God.

"Now therefore, our God—the great and mighty and awesome God, keeping covenant and steadfast love—do not treat lightly all the hardship that has come upon us, upon our kings, our officials, our priests, our prophets, our ancestors, and all your people, since the time of the kings of Assyria until today. You have been just in all that has come upon us, for you have dealt faithfully and we have acted wickedly; our kings, our officials, our priests, and our ancestors have not kept your law or heeded the commandments and the warnings that you gave them. Even in their own kingdom, and in the great goodness you bestowed on them, and in the large and rich land that you set before them, they did not serve you and did not turn from their wicked works. Here we are, slaves to this day—slaves in the land that you gave to our ancestors to enjoy its fruit and its good gifts. Its rich yield goes to the kings whom you have set over us because of our sins; they have power also over our bodies and over our livestock at their pleasure, and we are in great distress."

Doxology: The Language of Praise

This remembrance is voiced in a very particular form of speech innate to a people of thanksgiving and praise. This way of speech before God and others is called *doxology*, the language of blessing, praise and thanksgiving. The testimony of the awesome deeds that God has wrought is taken up in the language of doxology, "like the lover who delights in recounting the many good things the beloved has done."[11]

This testimony proclaims the people's true identity as a people embraced in lasting covenant. This speech moves beyond the current impasse. It all turns on the people's naming the ways God has been there in the past. They open themselves to God. The language of praise and thanksgiving directs us outward to God, who works wonders. To give thanks and praise to God moves us toward a total stripping of every alle-

---

Doxology

Praise, therefore, assumes and even evokes a world, a world where the affliction of the weak and the order of the universe are inextricably joined, where the provision of grass for animals and the securing of justice for one falsely accused are most clearly understood as manifestations of a single reality, the work of God. (On the world-making character of praise, see Walter Brueggemann, *Israel's Praise: Doxology against Idolatry and Ideology* [Philadelphia: Fortress, 1988].) It is a world where impossible things become possible, where things too difficult become the order of the day. We have noted in the hymns of praise the celebration of God's care of the weak in reversing the way things are, lifting up the lowly and putting down the mighty, feeding the hungry and giving sight to the blind, making the barren woman the joyous mother of children (e.g. 1 Samuel 2:1–10; Psalm 113). These are what Walter Brueggemann has aptly called "songs of impossibility," doxologies celebrating human impossibilities that have become God's possibilities. The praise of Israel bore witness to transformations and reversals of condition too wonderful for any human capability to bring off on its own or even to comprehend. In such reversals, all human definitions of the way things have to be in this world are challenged and overturned. The freedom and power of God say that what is laughable from a human perspective — see old Sarah's response to the announcement to Abraham that she would have a child! — is the way things are going to be when God is at work.

The Roots and Evolution of Eucharistic Praying

giance we might have to some other power or way of being; it explodes with hope.[12]

As Ezra names the God who forgives and never forgets, the people abandon any other claim they have and release themselves to the God who sets life in right order. "The very act of . . . recognizing that God is the only one on whom we can rely absolutely . . . is an act of faith that has the effect of putting us back in right relationship with God."[13] The people surrender themselves to the God whom they invoke to act again in their midst in decisive ways. And through their praise and thanksgiving, they let themselves go to the world, whose transformation they invoke in the certainty of God's faithfulness.[14]

The language of doxology, which is born of the people's remembrance and hope, shapes the various ways that the Jewish people speak to God. Upon waking in the morning or undertaking any task, when sitting

In a world that assumes the status is quo, that things have to be the way they are, and one must not assume too much about improving them, the doxologies of God's people are one of the fundamental indicators that wonders have not ceased, possibilities not yet dreamed of will happen, and hope is an authentic stance. That is ridiculous, of course—unless one has seen the wonders of God the past, the overthrow of the mighty and the setting free of an oppressed people, the gift of life in the face of death, fertility where there was barrenness. The resurrection truly defies all human categories and fits no epistemology, no ordinary philosophical, logical or scientific ways of knowing the truth. Yet Christians gather every Sunday to give praise to God for the impossible wonder that raised Christ from the dead. In its acts of doxology, the community of faith says to the world that all our presumptions about what can happen are overruled by the wonderful impossibilities that God's freedom and power have wrought.

Such praise is a powerful political act and, indeed, a subversive one. For it claims to know where justice and righteousness are to be found in the world, and they are not necessarily there where the world assumes. Praise declares that the Lord is turning this world upside down, reversing the order of power, casting down the mighty from their thrones. Praise of God, as one finds it in these many prayers of Scripture, is inherently a dangerous act, but always subject to being domesticated or simply neutralized. That can only happen, however, if the community of faith does not believe its own songs, does not believe that "God has done it!"

Excerpts from Patrick Miller, They Cried to the Lord *(Minneapolis: Augsburg Fortress, 1994), pp. 224–225. © 1994 Augsburg Fortress. Used with permission.*

down at table to eat, when gathered together for worship and even in time of tribulation, as the psalms show — there is no moment that is lived unaware of God's blessing and of the living relationship of the covenant forged in steadfast love and faithfulness. Every moment, "we give praise, honor, and glory to God because we find ourselves captivated by the sheer love and goodness of what God is or has done."[15]

THE PASCH: WHAT CHRISTIANS REMEMBER

We Christians are beholden to our Jewish ancestors, whose constant posture of praise, rich recourse to remembrance and poetic speech of doxology we inherited. Remembrance, praise, thanksgiving and supplication are part and parcel of who we are and what we do as Christians. For we Christians believe that in the fullness of time, God — the God who brought us from the abyss and delivered the Hebrew people from slavery, led them to the Promised Land and constantly reached out in mercy — sent the Son who took flesh and was born a human being, Jesus. He came, God's steadfast love and faithfulness enfleshed and visible to us, and turned the world on its end. To all who gathered near and listened, he announced, "The kingdom of God has come near; repent and believe." Jesus' proclamation "called into question the prevailing social and religious status quo: It opened the possibility of an alternative world, it held out the promise of establishing a different kind of community, it sought to bring out a new set of inclusive relationships."[16] Yet this world did not remain far off; it took flesh in their midst. Jesus gave sight to the blind. The lame he made leap. And the deaf became able to hear the voice of their God come near. Jesus blessed the poor, the weak, the persecuted.

The alternative world of forgiveness, the community of mutual love and the inclusive relationships took shape in astonishing ways as Jesus gathered the poor, the outcast and the sinners around the table to eat. To those so used to the ways of the world, this manifestation of the love of God in their midst, a love without stint, was scandalous. Jesus knew no bounds.

Though in the form of God,
Jesus did not claim
equality with God
but emptied himself,
taking the form of a slave,
human like one of us.

Flesh and blood,
he humbled himself,
obeying to the death,
death on a cross.

For this very reason
God lifted him high
and gave him the name
above all names.

So at the name of Jesus
every knee will bend
in heaven, on earth,
and in the world below,
and every tongue exclaim
to the glory of God the Father,
"Jesus Christ is Lord." Philippians 2:6–11

Jesus was obedient unto *death*. He was slapped and bruised, taunted and abandoned. He was nailed to a tree on Calvary, a trash heap outside the city. But it did not all end there, for the jaws of Death could not hold fast Life itself. Christ trampled death and shattered Satan's gates. Christ delivered us from slavery to freedom, from darkness to light, from mourning to joy, and raised us up to life forever. This Christ poured out the Spirit, the Spirit who gathers us from the corners of the earth and sanctifies us, to remain with us until the end. And the Spirit draws us to Christ, who intercedes for the world until that day of a new heaven and a new earth.

Passion, death, resurrection, mission of the Spirit and return: This is what is captured in the word *pasch*, the heart of our salvation wrought by God through Christ in the Spirit. And so it is that at the name of Jesus we bless God, who has blessed us through Christ and gathered us in the Spirit. Like Miriam, we are astounded that the wonders our God works are beyond our wildest imagination; we dance in praise and thanks. And as we do so, we make our very own the new life that is ours in God's extravagant love, and we call on God's Spirit to be all in all. Like Miriam, the women testify, "We have seen the Lord." Like Miriam, the disciples on the road to Emmaus announce, "We have seen the Lord." Both the women and the disciples on the road must announce to others what wonders they have come to know — like the psalmist of old and the prophet crying in the desert of disbelief.

Memory Kept at the Table

What more fitting place should there be for this proclamation than gathered at table for a meal. Throughout his ministry, Jesus gathered the wayward at table, and as they came together, they glimpsed the reign of God. And before he suffered death, he gathered his beloved once more around the table and commanded them to remember him — to assemble for a meal, to gather up all their fleshly memories of him, to free themselves to God's embrace of all human need, to manifest God's mercy, to lavish abundance on even the lowliest of God's people.[17] He commanded them to remember him — calling up memories of sacrifice, passover and exodus, covenant in blood, suffering servant and the reign to come.[18] He commanded them to remember him in the washing of feet and mutual love.[19] He commanded them to remember him until he comes again and all God's promises are tasted and all are drawn by the Spirit to the wedding feast in heaven, when God shall reign from everlasting to everlasting.[20]

Jesus' words and gestures at that meal serve as the basis for the Christian eucharist, for they communicate in a prophetic way the dynamic reality "of the whole event of Jesus' death and ultimate vindication," the reality of the pasch.[21] The first generation of Christians, still reeling from all that had transpired in Jerusalem, kept the memory of Jesus especially in the blessing and breaking of the bread and the sharing of the cup when they gathered on the first day of the week. True to their roots,

The Roots and Evolution of Eucharistic Praying

they gave thanks and praise for what God had done for them in Christ Jesus, which culminated in the pasch, the perfection of the covenant sealed in Christ's blood. And they pleaded that God remember them and Jesus' promises to be with them always in the Spirit and to return. Then they ate and drank.

While the witnesses are few and terse, they give us a hint that *eucharistia* — eucharist, thanksgiving — and gesture around the table were constitutive of Christian assembly. The assembly's memory and expectation of Jesus and their lives in Christ were summed up in their eucharist.

Of course, the diversity within the early community — from the Palestinian seacoast to the Syrian hinterland, from Rome to the North African shore — engendered a variety of ways in which the Christian people spoke and acted. The various Christian communities gave voice to their remembrance in thanks and praise, drawing on their many different images of Jesus and working these elements into the fabric of their cultural perceptions, linguistic styles and dominant attitudes.[22] From Rome in the second century, Justin, a philosopher and martyr, offers a tantalizing description of what Christians did on Sunday there: "We praise him by a word of prayer and thanksgiving, to the best of our ability, over all the things we offer."[23] Justin's description also tells us that the presider "gave thanks at length" over the bread and wine in memory of Jesus, to which the people "gave their assent by saying 'Amen.'"

In Justin's brief description, we learn several key points about eucharistic praying among Christians in Rome. First, they took up the language of doxology, addressed "to the Father of all, through the name of the Son and of the Holy Spirit."[24] Their Christian prayer was trinitarian. Their prayer extended what it received from its Jewish roots by naming the saving work of God through Jesus and the Spirit.

Second, eucharistic praying was marked by a certain freedom; it was extemporaneous but was guided by a received way of doing eucharist. The presider's "freedom to word the prayer each time . . . was not a freedom to pray at whim. His task was to utter *eucharistia,* to formulate once more a prayer of Christian praise and thanksgiving, filling in with his own words a pattern of prayer he learned in the continuous liturgical life of the community."[25]

Third, there was an ordered assembly in which the presider was charged with uttering the prayer of thanksgiving "to the best of his ability." But this prayer was indeed the prayer of all the assembly, in whose name the presider "sent up" the praises and whose assent was given at its conclusion.

THE EARLIEST SHAPE OF CHRISTIAN EUCHARISTIC PRAYING

Witnesses from other parts of the Christian world corroborate Justin's description and suggest that extemporaneity was characteristic of eucharistic praying in the first three centuries of Christianity. The early Christians had at their disposal the rich heritage of the people of Israel: the power of memory and the language of doxology. They called upon the outstanding moments of God's saving action and called on God to act once more in their midst, that Jesus be present to them in the breaking of the bread. The shape of their prayer was guided by the local conventions and done within limits forged by the received tradition.[26]

The church was constantly growing and changing in this early period, and likewise its forms and manners of praying changed and grew according to local need and the particular circumstances of the gathering. One leader might have been profoundly influenced by the psalms, another by table prayers. Each leader of prayer might have drawn on different events from the story of salvation, taken snippets of scriptural verses and local ways of phrasing, or maybe even borrowed from another neighboring church. Moreover, the locale of the gathering would influence the content. A prayer in the missionary byways or by ascetic preachers would surely be different from one by a leader in Rome or Alexandria. It is crucial to remember that in this time, "traditions, values and beliefs got their vitality from those who lived them and expressed them chiefly by the spoken word."[27]

Christians did their remembering the way their ancestors did: They discerned what was going on in the present situation and looked to how the future would be transformed because of the way God has saved. Also, this memory kept in prayer was embodied by the way Christians lived. As Acts of the Apostles tells it, Christian life was constituted by communion and service together with prayers and breaking of the bread (Acts 2:42–47). All of these things had to be taken together as witness to the Good News. And finally, we must keep in mind that the early Christian community's prayer of praise and thanksgiving made in memory of Jesus culminated in their eating and drinking the body and blood of Christ. "It is because the command of Christ to keep his memory is obeyed in the prayer of blessing over the bread and wine that these are transformed into his body and blood."[28] Our forebears in the faith understood the whole prayer as intimately connected with the transformation of the bread and wine, and at that only in connection with the whole of the liturgical action.

THE EVOLUTION OF FIXED PRAYERS

From these beginnings in guided freedom, the changing times and circumstances of church life led to the evolution of more fixed forms.[29] Still, the earliest written texts seem to have been offered as examples or suggestions for particular circumstances, not rigid prayers to be read. Even so, there emerged across the Christian world a desire for common elements, though the way these would be incorporated remained determined by local circumstances. The growth of Christianity and the more frequent gatherings also influenced the development of fixed prayers, or at least written texts, that could serve as a kind of memory aid or guide. And as the liturgy became more frequent and formal, especially in cities like Rome, the new surroundings and types of gatherings seemed to call for more formally composed prayers. Clearly, the pope's liturgy in a grand basilica in Rome demanded a different style of public prayer than did that of the presbyters in their smaller churches throughout the city.

At the same time, controversies arose that challenged what the Christian church believed about Jesus, God and the Holy Spirit. Councils convened to spell out with nuance and precision what was right belief. The church knew that what was being prayed in the assembly embodied what it meant to believe in the Christian God; so the local churches sought to ensure the expression of right belief and the more nuanced faith of the councils by writing down the best prayers for their presiders.

The churches in the major urban centers—Antioch, Alexandria, Edessa and Rome, for example—had particular influence on the smaller churches in the suburban and rural parts of their jurisdiction. In the fourth century, Jerusalem also became influential. Each of these churches developed particular conventions for eucharistic praying and particular ways of

A Third-Century Eucharistic Prayer

Priest The grace of our Lord Jesus Christ and the love of God the Father and the fellowship of the Holy Spirit be with us all, now and at all times and for ever and ever.

Response Amen.

Priest Let your hearts be on high.

Response To you, the God of Abraham and of Isaac and of Israel, the glorious King.

Priest The offering is being offered to God the Lord of all.

Response It is meet and right.

Deacon Peace be with us.

Priest Worthy of praise from every mouth and thanksgiving from every tongue is the adorable and glorious name of the Father and the Son and the Holy Spirit, who created the world in grace and its inhabitants in loving-kindness, and redeemed humankind in mercy and dealt very graciously with mortals.

Your majesty, my Lord, a thousand thousand heavenly beings and myriad myriads of angels adore and the hosts of spiritual beings, the ministers of fire and of spirit, glorifying your name with the cherubim and the holy seraphim, ceaselessly crying out and glorifying and calling to one another and saying:

Response Holy, holy, holy is the Lord Almighty:
the heavens and the earth are full of God's glory.
Hosanna in the highest! Hosanna to the Son of David!
Blessed is the one who has come and comes in the name of the Lord.
Hosanna in the highest!

Priest And with these heavenly hosts we give you thanks, my Lord, we also your unworthy, frail and miserable servants, because you have dealt very graciously with us in a way which cannot be repaid. You clothe yourself with our humanity to restore us to life by your divinity. You exalt our low estate, and raise up our fallen state, and resurrect our mortality, and forgive our sins, and acquit our sinfulness, and enlighten our understanding, and, our Lord and God, overcome our adversaries, and give victory to the unworthiness of our frail nature in the overflowing mercies of your grace. And for all your benefits and graces towards us we offer you glory and honour and thanksgiving and adoration now and at all times and for ever and ever.

Response   Amen.

Deacon   Pray in your hearts. Peace be with us.

Priest   My Lord, in your manifold and ineffable mercies, make a good and gracious remembrance for all the upright and just ancestors who were pleasing before you, in the commemoration of the body and blood of your Christ, which we offer to you upon the pure and holy altar, as you have taught us, and make with us your tranquillity and your peace all the days of the age, that all the inhabitants of the world may know you. You alone are God the true Father, and you sent our Lord Jesus Christ your Son and Beloved, and he, our Lord and our God, taught us in his life-giving Gospel all the purity and holiness of the prophets and apostles and martyrs and confessors and bishops and priests and deacons, and of all the children of the holy catholic church, those who have been signed with the sign of holy baptism.

And we also, O my Lord, your unworthy, frail, and miserable servants, who are gathered and stand before you, and have received by tradition the example which is from you, rejoicing and glorifying and exalting and commemorating and celebrating this great and awesome mystery of the passion and death and resurrection of our Lord Jesus Christ.

And let your Holy Spirit come, O my Lord, and rest upon this offering of your servants, and bless it and sanctify it that it may be to us, O my Lord, for the pardon of sins and for the forgiveness of shortcomings, and for the great hope of the resurrection from the dead, and for new life in the kingdom of heaven with all who have been pleasing before you.

And for all your wonderful dispensation which is towards us we give you thanks and glorify you without ceasing in your church redeemed by the precious blood of your Christ, with open mouths and unveiled faces, offering glory and honour and thanksgiving and adoration to your living and holy and life-giving name, now and at all times and for ever and ever.

Response   Amen.

Adapted from A. Gelston, The Eucharistic Prayer of Addai and Mari (Oxford: Clarendon Press, 1992), pp. 49–55. © 1992 Clarendon Press. Used with permission.

arranging their eucharistic prayer that no doubt reflected how these people believed in God; their prayers embodied the kinds of speech that these communities found to be particularly persuasive ways to keep memory. But even in their diversity, all drew on common memories of what God had done for them and sought to express what it meant to be saved by God in Christ and to ask for participation in God's life through the Spirit. A certain common vocabulary developed that cities exchanged with each other freely. Gradually, these prayers became standardized in urban hubs and were written down.

Thus, Christians developed particular styles of prayer through which they elaborated the language of praise, thanksgiving and supplication, and they expanded its basic dynamic. By the late fourth century, most Christian prayers came to include the Last Supper narrative, which grounded their remembrance with a clear reference to the scriptural command and promise of Christ. The hymn that begins "Holy, Holy, Holy," based on Isaiah 6 and borrowed from the synagogue, became a very popular way to express praise and thanks, and was eventually added. The supplication dimension, the plea that God act once more, began to ask God "to let the Holy Spirit come" or "to send the Holy Spirit." And they detailed what they wanted God to transform in more detailed petitions.

The people would most likely have chanted in some fashion the "Holy, Holy" hymn and given their final "Amen," which the Fathers of the church emphasize greatly. Though information is sketchy, it is likely that the bishop, or presbyter in his place, chanted or cantillated at least parts of the prayer, if not the entire prayer. It is not until later centuries that we get better clues as to the prayer's performance.

Thus, extemporaneous prayers gave way to memorized ones or ones proclaimed from written texts. When it came down to composing prayers, the various churches made clever use of the tradition that they had received. In some places, the editors gathered together existing material and arranged it according to the way the local church framed its prayer. In other places, simpler, earlier material was expanded to meet new needs. In still others, pieces from other cities' prayers or from other eucharistic prayers were slotted into their existing prayers to create new versions.[30] How they composed the prayers, what they wrote, and how they wrote it were all dependent on the local culture and popular need. For example, in the church of East Syria (present-day Iraq), the eucharistic prayer of Addai and Mari speaks of God's gracious dealing with a humanity besieged by sin and frailty, takes up the popular images of putting on clothing as a way to talk about salvation, and uses strong future-oriented language to call upon the Holy Spirit.

Meanwhile, the Roman church seems to have developed a eucharistic prayer that drew more deeply on the cultic language and prayer styles of the traditional, late-antique-Roman temple priesthood and brotherhoods.[31] The Roman church's prayer was also influenced by that church's unique qualities, called the "genius" of the Roman church: its "simplicity, practicality, great sobriety and self-control, gravity and dignity . . . but not the creative imagination."[32] We still see in the composition and recording of prayers the desire to express the church's faith grounded in the saving acts of God in Christ.

RETAINING A BREADTH OF PRAYERS

The legacy of the extemporaneous prayer — the imaginative recall and casting of the events of salvation — stayed with the churches even as the eucharistic prayer moved to fixed texts. Interestingly, the churches in the East and West came to accommodate variety in different ways because of their different circumstances. In the East, the churches opted for a great number of different eucharistic prayers. The Byzantine church adopted two eucharistic prayers, one ascribed to St. John Chrysostom and the other to St. Basil; the Syriac-speaking churches of the West have at least 80 different eucharistic prayers; the East Syrians preserve three; the Ethiopians around 20; the Coptic church today uses three; and the Armenian Church had ten. In some of these churches, there were late campaigns to compose eucharistic prayers, but for the most part the variety of prayers results from older ones being borrowed from church to church and adapted "because of their intrinsic merits, because of the prestige of the church from which they come or because of the (often fictious) prestigious name they bear"—not variety for variety's sake.[33]

Western Christians developed another way to preserve the spirit of variability. The churches in Gaul, Spain and Italy wanted solemn, carefully crafted Latin prayers that had flourish. For the increasing number of presbyters who knew little Latin, those demands made improvisation difficult, especially when they needed texts for the increasing number of special feasts and commemorations in the liturgical cycle.[34] In Gaul and Spain, instead of composing many whole eucharistic prayers, the leaders of prayer opted to devise a prayer that had certain sections that stayed the same no matter what the Sunday or feast and certain sections that could change depending on which Sunday of the year it was or which feast was being celebrated.

The more reserved liturgy of the Romans, particularly that of the bishop of Rome, did not share their neighbors' exuberance. The Romans preserved the language of praise and thanksgiving in the opening section of their prayer, which changed according to Sunday or feast, and occasionally made some minor changes in the rest of the prayer if the occasion was particularly significant. This way, they could still make explicit recall of the marvels that God had done, even if they were writ small in terms of the feast or person of the day. This variable first section was called the "preface," a word that originally referred to a public proclamation, not something that comes before something else, as we use it today. The rest of the Roman prayer was intensely supplicatory, and this section of the prayer became for the most part fixed. On certain major feasts or occasions, slight variations would be inserted.

A LONG WAY FROM MIRIAM'S SHORE

Eventually, however, the way that the eucharistic prayer was understood and prayed shifted, often in peculiar ways. In the West, some of the seed for the shift in eucharistic praying was sown when the liturgy was not

The Roots and Evolution of Eucharistic Praying

adapted to the evolving languages of the people. Previously, the assembly, in whose name the presbyter prayed, lifted up praise and thanksgiving in remembrance of the pasch and called on the Spirit. Soon, though, the language of the prayer itself became an obstacle to their involvement. They spoke one language, while the liturgy persisted in another. With the turn to written texts that were read, the people began to sense that the prayer was less and less their business — they could not understand what was being said. It seemed as if the prayer was the business of the leader, who could read the written text or memorize it.

The person who could read the text found therein language that fostered a perception that the prayer was the domain of the professional cleric. As we saw, the language of the Roman eucharistic prayer is reminiscent of pagan cultic language, which perhaps influenced its development. Also, the language of praise and thanksgiving could be found only in the short variable section, while the bulk of the prayer focused on beseeching God — intercession. The Roman prayer also used images of sacrifice and offering. While the language of sacrifice is quite traditional in Christian understanding, originally it was used to speak of Christian worship as "indeed true worship and that it is the new worship of those redeemed in Christ."[35] Moreover, the language of sacrifice was used to describe the whole of Christian life and worship; it was a way of speaking richly about them. However, especially with the echoes of temple sacrifice, the rich and varied meanings of sacrifice became more narrow and reduced. So, too, would the understanding of the whole of the eucharistic action.

They had come a long, long way from Miriam's dance on the shore, from the great prayer of Ezra, from the singing of the psalms and the thanksgiving at meals, and from Justin's assembly where the presbyter gave thanks to the best of his ability. It looked, sounded and felt very different. But buried therein, the eucharistic prayer still expressed the church's remembrance of the events that restored grace, looking forward to eternal life and asking for a present share in the saving love of God in ways that were culturally and historically meaningful.[36]

In due time, most of the eucharistic prayer came to be prayed in such a low voice by the bishop or presbyter that the people could not even hear it. An order for the pope's celebration of the liturgy from the eighth century gives us a look at how praying the eucharistic prayer had changed. After the pope chanted the preface, everyone took up the singing of the Holy, Holy, with body bowed. Meanwhile, the order directs that the pope alone rise and "enter quietly into the canon" while the chant of the people continued.[37] It was probably so quiet that only those around the pope could hear, even when the singing had finished. The rest of the eucharistic prayer was imaged as a "sanctuary," a kind of sacred space into which the bishop or presbyter alone could go. The understanding of the role of the

The Christian Sacrifice

If the purpose of sacrifice is carefully circumscribed . . . if worship and the moral life are invited by the talk of "offering" into self-giving, if such self-giving acts are seen as reflecting and celebrating the all-sufficient self-gift of Christ rather than in any sense adding to it, the language can be and has been used to speak the Christian gospel. Much Christian energy and anger have been expended on interconfessional struggles about how to get this syntax just right. Underneath those struggles, the shared, ecumenical intuition has been that the death of Christ, the meaning of Christian worship and the orientations of Christian ethics are all deeply connected. "Sacrifice" has been valued as one important way to talk about that connection.

The surprise has been missing, however. Christian worship is not sacrifice. Neither was the death of Christ, at least when it is looked at as a historical event. Neither is the moral life. Christian ethics are about the loving service of the neighbor and care of the world, quite secular affairs. Christ's death was a public execution; while it may have been marked by some grisly ritual characteristics, it was thoroughly alien to the sacred cultic exchange. According to the New Testament, his death was "outside the camp" (Hebrews 13:11–13); it was unclean and a "curse"(Galations 3:13). Moreover, Christian worship is baptism next to word next to meal — these simply are not sacrifice. It is hard for us to say this, inured as we are to the conventional character of such speech, to the meanings of worship we have commonly drawn from such speech, and to the generations of confessional identity that have depended on each group's peculiar use of such speech. But facing this *no* is important for a renewed understanding of the relationship of worship both to Jesus' death and to ethics. Facing this *no* is important for a new ecumenical approach to the primary theology of the assembly.

The application of the cultic terminology to ethics might be explainable as spiritualization. It could be a Christian use of a long tradition of Hebrew thought that had spiritualized the meaning of the temple cult, making "sacrifice" available to describe the interior state of one who praised God and kept the law: ". . . you have no delight in sacrifice; if I were to give a burnt offering, you would not be pleased. The sacrifice acceptable to God is a broken spirit; a broken and contrite heart, God, you will not despise," says the psalmist (Psalm 51:16 – 17). The prophet echoes the sentiment: "Will the Lord be pleased with thousands of rams, with ten thousands of rivers of oil? Shall I give my firstborn for my transgression, the fruit of my body for the sin of my soul? . . . what does the Lord require of you but to do justice, and to love kindness, and to walk humbly with your God" (Micah 6:7 – 8). Precisely such reflections made the keeping of the law available in the Jewish Diaspora, away from Jerusalem and the cult, to great lay movements apart from the sacerdotal structure of the temple. Such reflections, in the scriptures and among the rabbis, may very well have been useful also to Christians in reflecting on the moral life.

One might say that such a spiritualization is what is intended in the application of this language also to Christian worship and to the death of Christ. The interior state, the self-gift, of both Jesus and the worshiper is the matter of import brought to expression in calling the cross and the action of the assembly sacrifice. The problem is that early Christian texts that use this language (see, for example, 1 Corinthians 5:7 for Christ as the Passover sacrifice and 1 Corinthians 3:10 – 17 for the assembly in the Spirit as temple") are not concerned with interior states but with the bare fact of Jesus' death or with the actual proceedings at a Christian gathering and with their meaning for us. The accent here, and in other texts, does not fall on individual, ethical motivation, whether of Christ or of the believer, but on meaning.

It is better to say that sacrifice is the wrong word in these cases, but that is just the point. "Sacrifice" is used metaphorically when it is applied to the death of Christ or to the Christian assembly. (See David N. Power, "Words That Crack: The Uses of 'Sacrifice' in Eucharistic Discourse," *Worship* 53 [1979]: 386 – 404) Metaphor, the "transposition of an alien name," (Aristotle, *Poetics* 1457b:6 – 9) intends to use the wrong word in order to reveal to the imagination a plurality of meanings that otherwise could not be spoken. A dialogue between "this cannot be so!" and "how is this so?" is meant to be created in the minds of the hearers. Such metaphor, in liturgical use, is yet another example of biblical rhetoric alive in the communal assembly. The wrongness of the word needs to be heightened, not tamed, in order for the figure of speech to work. We need to inquire what truth about God is proposed by our calling our assembly action sacrifice when it is not. . . .

Excerpts from Gordon Lathrop, Holy Things: A Liturgical Theology *(Minneapolis: Augsburg Fortress, 1993), pp. 139 – 142. Copyright © 1993, Augsburg Fortress. Reprinted with permission.*

whole assembly in the action and of the intimate connection between our offering thanks and God's remembering us in transforming love were weakened. The ritual emphasis began to fall exclusively on God's coming in sacred mystery, which fostered a sense of awe that called for silence.[38]

In the East, the shift to a silent prayer in an atmosphere of awe took place earlier, around the sixth century. However, at the same time, acclamations and biddings by the deacon began to be inserted into the prayers. While the first part of the eucharistic prayer continued to be prayed aloud in the West, in the East the presider prayed it in a low voice while the people expanded the "It is right to give our thanks and praise" into a song that lasted to the Holy, Holy. The priest would continue quietly and raise his voice at certain moments (or the deacon would give a bidding), and the people would respond. While they may have been intended to keep the attention of the people, whose minds no doubt wandered once the prayer became the domain of the priest, the acclamations became so complex that the choir took over many of them. The professional singers elaborated the music, and soon the people were left with little to call their own.[39]

The Westerners, of whom we are direct descendants, went an entirely different direction when the prayer fell into silence. Here, only the oldest level of acclamations remained: the introductory dialogue, the Holy, Holy and the Amen. The deacons never got in on the act, and in some places, the choirs would sing hymns that had no relation to the eucharistic prayer at all![40] There was never the development of the multiple acclamation that the more exuberant East would come to include. Before long, monks would be directed to pray the Lord's Prayer over and over, or all or part of the psalms. The people took to devotional prayers, which became for them powerful means for remembering the great pasch of Jesus in a way that the official prayer could not for them. Perhaps even more ironic was the development of devotional prayers for the priest himself that apparently "better responded to his own devotion than the official text."[41] The priest recited the official prayer quietly, the people prayed their own prayer, and the priest made his devotions to the side of the assembly's. While the "priest was everyone's voice . . . it no longer expresse[d] their common prayer but prayer in which their own tended simply to become parallel."[42]

CHANGING UNDERSTANDINGS

Overarching the early medieval developments was the influence of the Germanic cultures on the Christian worldview and the Roman liturgical celebration. The Germanic peoples infused the liturgy with their more objectified way of understanding the world. Concrete material things or examples were more important to the Germanic peoples; they had, after all, been steeped in a magical worldview before being brought into the Christian world.[43] So increasing attention was given to relics, the eucharistic elements and miracles.

Grappling with the impact of the Germanic cultures, the medieval church also shifted its understanding of the liturgical action. Given that the people's language and the liturgy's language grew further apart and that the presider was praying the text in a quiet voice, about all people could do was watch. The eucharistic prayer became "a rite of priestly ministry, to which the faithful looked as to an expression of holiness in their midst."[44] They could observe the actions of the priest, which commentaries on the Mass began to explain in fantastic dramatic terms, drawing on the life of Christ for examples. People liked good drama. Participation in the eucharistic prayer became more a matter of watching what the priest did and engaging in devotional prayer.

As controversies arose in the later Middle Ages over what it meant to say that the bread and wine were the Body and Blood of Christ, attention fixed on parts of the supper, or institution, narrative: "This is my Body" *(Hoc est enim Corpus meum)* and "This is (the cup of) my Blood" *(Hic est enim calix sanguinis mei)*. While some might still nod in the direction of the whole eucharistic prayer as being necessary, most considered it mere decoration.[45] The great medieval mindset that sought precision and still bore traces of a magical worldview wanted to pinpoint the moment, to find the minimum requirements, something culturally relevant at the time. The words of Christ in the institution narrative became the heart of the matter. They were identified as the "words of consecration." Christ's words, recorded in the gospels, were believed to do what they said. When spoken by the priest, because he was understood to be acting in the person of Christ, the high priest, they were considered effective.

These developments furthered the divorce between the assembly's action and the priest's action. The assembled people offered "through the hands of the priest" because he acted as Christ. The priest's action was thus viewed as having a purpose in itself quite apart from the people. The Mass was something that the priest did "for or on behalf of the people rather than together with them."[46] The priest mediated between God and the people, seeking pardon for their sins, special grace in time of need or help for the dead in the act of offering sacrifice. [47]

The people's posture and their devotion changed in response to these new understandings. The customary postures of standing and bowing gave way to kneeling, the posture for personal prayer, not liturgical action. In some cases, people knelt with arms outstretched in the prayer position. Seeing the Body and Blood of Christ took on increased importance for the people's devotion, and the desire to gaze upon the Lord's Body "was the driving force" that led to the introduction of the gesture of elevation at the institution narrative. It was an "intrusion of a very notable innovation into the canon which for ages had been regarded as an inviolable sanctuary."[48] Eventually, kneeling to honor the elevated Body and Blood of Christ took hold, and even in the end won out over looking at the elements, as folks began to kneel with head bowed.[49] Kneeling was a posture for their intense supplicatory private prayer and adoration.

REFORM

In short, while the texts of the eucharistic prayer remained unchanged, what did change was how that prayer was prayed and understood. The great eucharistic prayer was no longer the way that the people gave thanks for their redemption or remembered the mighty deeds of God in Christ. The climax of the liturgy was now the "priestly consecration and offering, and the elevation of the host."[50] The people entered into the eucharist through devotions, stipends and hearing Mass — a far cry from the shouts of "Amen!" to their thanksgiving prayer that shook many an ancient church.[51] The Holy, Holy became the fare of elaborate choral singing, and the hush of the canon was broken by ringing bells to call people's attention to the priest's actions, his back turned to them as they knelt with heads bowed. It is no wonder that all manner of superstitious practices crept in.

The reformers reacted vehemently to the way that the eucharistic prayer had come to be understood, the way it was prayed and the prevailing theology of the eucharist. Luther, for example, wanted to "repudiate everything that smacks of sacrifice, together with the entire canon and retain only that which is pure and holy."[52] Luther sought thus to restore a simple thanksgiving with the Last Supper narrative. In some other reformers' work, the eucharistic prayer was either abandoned in favor of just the Last Supper narrative, reworked to simplify the prayer or replaced with lengthy prayers surrounding the Last Supper narrative. Cranmer, for example, reworked the traditional Roman Canon. The Council of Trent, in defending the Catholic faith against the arguments and changes of the Reformers, "established the medieval eucharist as the core of Catholic practice for four more centuries."[53] It was not until our own century, with the convening of the Second Vatican Council, that the way of eucharistic praying was radically transformed — indeed shaken back to its roots.

NOTES

1. Lawrence A. Hoffmann, "Rabbinic Berakhah and Jewish Spirituality," in *Asking and Thanking,* Concilium 1990/3, ed. C. Duquoc and C. Florestan (Philadelphia: Trinity Press International, 1990), 27.

2. Patrick D. Miller, They Cried Unto the Lord: The *Form and Theology of Biblical Prayer* (Minneapolis, Minn.: Augsburg Fortress, 1994), 190.

3. Miller, 225.

4. Miller, 227.

5. Miller, 217–218.

6. Walter Brueggemann, *The Prophetic Imagination* (Philadelphia: Fortress Press, 1978), 69–70.

7. See W. Brueggemann, *Israel's Praise: Doxology against Idolatry and Ideology* (Philadelphia: Fortress 1988), 34–53.

8. See David N. Power, *The Eucharistic Mystery: Revitalizing the Tradition* (New York: Crossroad, 1992), 43–50.

9. D. Power, "When Words Fail: The Function of Systematic Theology in Liturgical Studies," Proceedings of the North *American Academy of Liturgy* (1991): 24 and *Eucharistic Mystery,* 304–311.

10. Jean-Luc Marion, *God Without Being,* trans. T. A. Carlson (Chicago: University of Chicago Press, 1991), 172–173.

11. Catherine Mowry Lacugna, God For Us: The Trinity *and Christian Life* (San Francisco: Harper-Collins, 1991), 335.

12. Brueggemann, *Prophetic Imagination* 69–73.

13. LaCugna, 335.

14. See D. Power, Unsearchable Riches: The Symbolic Nature of Liturgy (New York: Pueblo, 1984), 164–165 and "Sacraments: Symbolizing God's Power in the Church," CTSA Proceedings 37 (1982): 64.

15. LaCugna, 335.

16. Dermot Lane, Keeping Hope Alive (New York: Paulist 1996), 94.

17. Nathan Mitchell, Eucharist as Sacrament of Initiation, Forum Essays 2 (Chicago: Liturgy Training Publications, 1994), 97–104.

18. D. Power, "Eucharist," in Systematic Theology: Roman Catholic Perspectives, vol. II, ed. F. Schüssler Fiorenza and J. Galvin (Minneapolis: Fortress, 1991), 268, and Eucharistic Mystery, 51–57.

19. On the two traditions, cultic and testamentary, see Xavier Léon-Dufour, Sharing Eucharistic Bread: The Witness of the New Testament (New York: Paulist Press, 1987).

20. See J. Reumann, The Supper of the Lord (Philadelphia: Fortress, 1985), 23–26, and Lane, 198–200.

21. See J. Meier, "The eucharist at the Last Supper: Did it happen?" Theological Digest 42:4 (Winter 1995): 347–350.

22. See D. Power, "Eucharist,"

23. Justin Martyr, First Apology 13.2, trans. in Prayers of the Eucharist: Early and Reformed (hereafter PEER), ed. R.C.D. Jasper and G. J. Cuming (New York: Pueblo, 1987), 28.

24. First Apology, 65; PEER 28.

25. A. Bouley, From Freedom to Formula: The Evolution of the Eucharistic Prayer from Oral Improvisation to Written Texts, Catholic University of America Studies in Christian Antiquity, 21 (Washington, D.C.: Catholic University of America Press, 1981), 116.

26. Bouley, 152.

27. Bouley, 153.

28. Power, "Eucharist," 274.

29. This paragraph depends on Bouley, 246–264.

30. See J. Fenwick, Fourth Century Anaphoral Construction Techniques, Grove Liturgical Study, 45 (Bramcote, Nottingham: Grove Books, 1986); and the remarks of B. Spinks, The Sanctus in the Eucharistic Prayer (Cambridge, England: Cambridge University Press, 1991), 108–111.

31. See H. A. J. Wegman, "Genealogie des Eucharistiegebetes," Archiv für Liturgiewissenschaft 33 (1991): 215–216.

32. From the renowned essay by E. Bishop, "The Genius of the Roman Rite," in Liturgica Historica (Oxford, 1918), 12.

33. Bouley, 252.

34. Bouley, 194–195.

35. Power, Mystery, 142.

36. Power, Mystery, 140.

37. Josef Jungmann, The Mass of the Roman Rite: Its Origins and Development, volume II (Westminster, Md.: Christian Classics, 1986), 138–140.

38. See the remarks of Jungmann, 101.

39. See L. Bouyer, Eucharist: Theology and Spirituality of the Eucharistic Prayer (Notre Dame, Ind.: University of Notre Dame Press, 1968), 374–376.

40. Bouyer, 377.

41. Bouyer, 377.

42. Bouyer, 377.

43. See A. Mirgeler, Mutations of Western Christianity (Notre Dame, Ind., and London: University of Notre Dame Press, 1968), 44–65; and James C. Russell, The Germanization of Early Medieval Christianity (New York: Oxford, 1994).

44. Power, Mystery, 134–135.

45. See Thomas Talley, "Eucharistic Prayers, Past Present and Future," Revising the Eucharist: Groundwork for the Anglican Communion, Alcuin/GROW Liturgical Study 27, ed. David R. Holeton (Bramcote, Nottingham: Grove Books, 1994), 10–11; and Pierre-Marie Gy, La Liturgie dans l'histoire (Paris: Cerf, 1990), 214–215.

46. Power, "Eucharist," 276–277.

47. See Power, Mystery, 164–171.

48. Jungmann, 208.

49. See Jungmann, 211–212.

50. Power, Mystery, 202.

51. See Power, Mystery, 183 on the people's devotion and piety.

52. Martin Luther, Formula Missae et communionis, in PEER 192.

53. Power, "Eucharist," 279.

THE RECOVERY OF THE EUCHARISTIC PRAYER

hen Pope John XXIII sounded the clarion call to council, the Roman church had been praying a single eucharistic prayer for well over 400 years. This prayer was ordinarily valued for only a section of its words, and it was entrusted entirely to the priest, with some singing by the choir as a possible backdrop.

Already in the nineteenth century, the stirrings of the liturgical movement had given impetus to exploration and reform of the way the church celebrated. The great historians of liturgy recovered and translated texts that had been unknown to the generations before them, and the burgeoning study of the church Fathers recovered homilies and letters that showed a lively and rich theology of liturgy and the sacraments. Pope Pius X opened the way for renewal by calling for more frequent, even daily, communion. After the Second World War, Pius XII drew attention to the importance of worship and urged active participation in it by all the people. The monumental work of the bishops at Vatican II drew from this treasury while at the same time remaining ever conscious of the complex cultural situation of the church in the modern world.

Among the many reforms and challenges of the Council were two interrelated developments that have had tremendous impact on the recovery of the eucharistic prayer from centuries of disfigurement: an understanding of the church and an understanding of the liturgy. The Council offered new perspectives on what it means to be church. The church is described as the beloved people of God, redeemed by Christ and made holy by the Spirit. "The baptized, by regeneration and the anointing of the Holy Spirit, are consecrated as a spiritual house and a holy priesthood, that through all their Christian activities they may offer spiritual sacrifices and proclaim the marvels of him who has called them out of darkness into his wonderful light."[1] The whole people of God bears witness to the world of the love and saving work of God. All the baptized "have been made sharers in their own way in the priestly, prophetic and kingly office of Christ" (LG, 31).

The Council emphasized that the people of God form the one Body of Christ, under Christ the Head in the unity of his Spirit (LG, 13). Joined together in the same faith, baptized into the one Christ Jesus, gathered at the one table in the one Spirit, the believers form the one Body of Christ in the world. All is done, as St. Paul urged the Corinthians, for the building up of that Body (see 1 Corinthians 14:26–31). While the ordained exercise a special role in forming and leading the priestly people, all the baptized united share in the one priesthood of Christ. They exercise that priesthood when they share in the offering of the eucharist along with the presbyter: "All have their own part to play in the liturgical action" (LG, 10). All the baptized exercise "that priesthood, too . . . by prayer and thanksgiving, by the witness of a holy life, self-denial and active charity" (LG, 10). Such are the components of the priestly office of the baptized.

In previous times, our understanding of church tended to focus exclusively on "the institutional dimension of the church: the identification and distribution of authority."[2] The church was equated with its leaders. The Council pointed out that what makes the church the church is the call of God, which gathers us together; the word of Christ, which summons us to faith; the grace of the Spirit, which unites us and makes us holy; the sacramental communion of faith, hope and love, which transforms us; and the apostolic ministry, through which we witness to the world.[3] The church is not some abstract or removed entity but comes to be in the gathering of local assemblies of the baptized. It is when gathered around the communion table under the ministry of the bishop or the bishop's representative that the local community manifests itself as the Body of Christ: "Christ is present through whose power and influence the one, holy, catholic and apostolic church is constituted. For sharing in the

*The whole church
gathers and
actively celebrates
the liturgy; no
one is a spectator*

Body and Blood of Christ has no other effect that to accomplish our transformation into that which we receive" (LG, 26).

This understanding of the church—as the manifestation of the risen Christ in the world through the priestly activity of the baptized—is intertwined with the second outstanding conciliar development: the role and nature of liturgy. Every liturgical celebration is an action of Christ and Christ's Body, the church.[4] Thus, when the church gathers to celebrate the liturgy, especially the eucharist, because the liturgy is an action of Christ, the Head and the Body, the "work of our redemption takes place . . . and the faithful express in their lives and portray to others the mystery of Christ and the real nature of true church" (SC, 2). The whole church gathers and actively celebrates the liturgy; no one is a spectator.

The Council emphasizes that "the principal manifestation of the church consists in the full, active participation of all God's holy people in the same liturgical celebrations, especially in the same eucharist, in one prayer, at one altar" at which the bishop or the bishop's representative presides (SC, 41). The purpose of the liturgical celebration of the sacraments is threefold: to sanctify people, to build up the Body of Christ and to worship God (SC, 59). It is never the priest's Mass or the priest's prayer but the worship of the whole Body, ordained priest and people together to the praise and glory of God's name. The celebration of the eucharist is not what the priest does on behalf of the baptized, but what all the baptized do together (SC, 48).

We are most profoundly who we are as church when we gather on Sunday to offer our thanks and praise to God in the celebration of the eucharist. We are most profoundly who we are as baptized Christians in our gathering at the table of the Lord's Body and Blood. We are most profoundly who we are when animated by the Holy Spirit, who sanctifies us and bears our prayers before the throne of grace. Yet the Council called the liturgy the "source and summit" of the church's power and activity

Who Prays the Eucharistic Prayer?

The eucharistic prayer is the prayer of the faithful. As presider in the gathering, the priest voices that prayer, but does so as the tongue of the Body: It must be (and be experienced as) the prayer of the whole Body of Christ coming before the Father with praise and thanksgiving. The presider's manner must not suggest any withdrawal from the assembly at this point but rather, as leader in prayer, an intensified solidarity with them in Christ. Introductory dialogue, tone of voice, facial expression, posture, gestures, manner of eye contact — all these may be used effectively to maintain the unity of the assembly in a unified prayer. The attitude of presider and people and the style with which the acclamations are done should indicate clearly that these are parts of the prayer, not interrup-

tions, interventions, or decorations. Congregational attention and involvement must be maintained and extended by developing the dialogic character of the prayer, but participation includes the visual and kinesthetic senses as well as verbal and auditory forms.

What is the thrust of the praying? The eucharistic outlook is one of corporate gratitude publicly expressed on humanity's behalf, not petition or propitiation. When people come to recognize that they are redeemed, they have not thereby lost the sense of sin but rather are grateful because they realize the situation they would have been in were it not for Christ. Eucharistic prayer (in the wide sense) is thus the central movement of all Christian prayer. Eucharistic prayer (in the more specific sense) is

(SC, 10), not the "be all and end all." The life of conversion, prayer and mission flow from the liturgy and lead one back to liturgy in praise and thanks to God.

A New Departure for Rome

It is in this context that we can situate the reform of the liturgy and the reclaiming of eucharistic praying and communion. Because the church is the manifestation of the risen Christ in the world, and because its liturgy is the church's outstanding means of witness to the world of its identity, then how that Body prays and what words and gestures it takes up matter a great deal. While the *Constitution on the Sacred Liturgy* did not specifically take up the eucharistic prayer, the implementation of its calls to reform the eucharistic prayer became a major concern.

essentially a heartfelt public acknowledgment of gratitude and thanksgiving to God for what has happened to and for us in Christ, for what is happening and for what will happen.

But what does it mean for us to praise God publicly? There is clearly a difference between public and private praise. Both may, of course, be merely matters of politeness or flattery or even insincerity, but generally to praise someone publicly is to let the world know where one stands. Particularly when the object of one's praise is not universally acknowledged or when such praise will lead to specific expectations of the one praising or even impose certain obligations and responsibilities, then public praise becomes a public commitment of one's person. The eucharistic prayer, if it is *meant*, is consequently a responsible confession of faith—indeed, it is, after baptism, the central Christian profession of faith.

In what context do we praise God? Our praise of God in the eucharistic prayer is our public acknowledgment of gratitude for all that is ours in Christ and our commitment to the eucharistic way of life. This way of life is necessarily communal and corporate and so requires the Christian community itself to reach beyond its boundaries to find its purpose for existence. The context within which the praise of God is publicly proclaimed shows this. The eucharistic prayer is the Christian community's table prayer. The gesture of the shared meal itself makes a statement and issues a challenge, but the words of the prayer which precedes it and states its nature and purpose make it unmistakable: All the world is gift to us and in sharing it with one another we give thanks to God.

Excerpts from James Dallen, "Spirituality of Eucharistic Prayer," Worship 58 (1984): pp. 368–370. © 1984 James Dallen. Used with permission.

"For the sake of greater richness and variety, many . . . have had the desire that, while retaining the traditional and revered Roman Canon, the Latin church, like other churches, should have other eucharistic prayers as well. By papal mandate the Consilium has therefore prepared

A Fourth-Century Eucharistic Prayer

The deacons shall present the offering to [the bishop]; and he, laying hands on it with all the presbytery, shall give thanks, saying:

> The Lord be with you.
> And with your spirit.
> Up with your hearts.
> We have them with the Lord.
> Let us give thanks to the Lord.
> It is fitting and right.

And then the bishop shall continue thus:

We render thanks to you, O God, through your beloved child Jesus Christ, whom in the last times you sent to us as saviour and redeemer and angel of your will; who is your inseparable Word, through whom you made all things, and in whom you were well pleased. You sent him from heaven into the Virgin's womb. Conceived in the womb, he was made flesh and was manifested as your Son, being born of the Holy Spirit and the Virgin. Fulfilling your will and gaining for you a holy people, he stretched out his hands when he should suffer, that he might release from suffering those who have believed in you.

And when he was betrayed to voluntary suffering that he might destroy death, and break the bonds of the devil, and tread down hell, and shine upon the righteous, and fix a term, and manifest the resurrection, he took bread and gave thanks to you, saying, "Take, eat; this is my body, which shall be broken for you." Likewise also the cup, saying, "This is my blood, which is shed for you; when you do this, you make my remembrance."

Remembering therefore his death and resurrection, we offer to you the bread and the cup, giving you thanks because you have held us worthy to stand before you and minister to you. And we ask that you would send your Holy Spirit upon the offering of your holy church; that, gathering [them] into one, you would grant to all who partake of the holy things to partake of the fullness of the Holy Spirit for the strengthening of faith in truth, that we may praise and glorify you through your child Jesus Christ, through whom be glory and honour to you, with the Holy Spirit, in your holy church, both now and to the ages of ages. Amen.

Excerpts from Geoffrey J. Cuming, Hippolytus: A Text for Students with Introduction, Translation, Commentary and Notes. *Grove Liturgical Studies 8. (Bramcote, Nottingham: Grove Books Ltd., 1991), pp. 10–11.*

three new eucharistic prayers, supplementing them with an expanded series of prefaces."[5] And so the Roman church's centuries-old practice of using a single prayer with a few variable prefaces gave way. The intention of the conciliar reform hearkens to the nature of the eucharistic prayer as the central Christian prayer of thanksgiving and supplication. "The Holy See has introduced three new anaphoras into the Roman liturgy . . . in the interest of making possible in the central part of the eucharistic celebration a better proclamation of God's blessings and a better recollection of the history of salvation."[6] (*Anaphora*, which means "offering," is another word for the eucharistic prayer.)

Interestingly, Rome borrowed and adapted prayers — strategies we saw at work in the great churches of the past. The Roman eucharistic prayer, or Roman Canon, as it was known, was slightly revised to become Eucharistic Prayer I. Eucharistic Prayer II is an adaptation of an old prayer from the *Apostolic Tradition* — an example of prayer reputed to reflect a usage of the church at Rome in perhaps the fourth century — with distinctive Roman material slotted in. However, rather than being a fixed prayer, it was devised to allow for the variable prefaces — a particular Western trademark. Eucharistic Prayer III is a new composition based on the first eucharistic prayer, and it also allows the Roman preference for variable prefaces that name specific details of salvation history in the course of the liturgical year. The fourth prayer is an adaptation of an ancient Eastern prayer attributed to St. Basil and is different from the other three. Like the Eastern eucharistic prayers, it does not allow for variable prefaces according to the feast but is an unchanging, fixed prayer.

In the years after the promulgation of the Roman Missal, five other eucharistic prayers appeared: three for Masses with children and two that focus on the theme of reconciliation. After a period of trial use, they were incorporated into the Roman Missal. More recently, a prayer that originally had been composed for a synod of Swiss bishops and had been adopted in European countries has been translated into English and is now permitted for Masses for Various Needs and Occasions, bringing the number of approved prayers in English to ten.

The reform of eucharistic praying not only sought to restore the centrality of the prayer of thanksgiving and supplication but also demonstrated what we have seen from history. The eucharistic prayer takes up the beliefs, the memories and the hopes of a given Christian assembly and expresses them

Zaire Rite

The following is a version of the eucharistic prayer put forth for approval for use by the dioceses of Zaire.

The announcer strikes his/her gong and says to the people:
Brothers and sisters, let us listen attentively.

All remain in silence for a moment. Then a dialogue begins between the presider and the assembly.

P: The Lord be with you.

A: And with your spirit.

P: Let us raise our heart.

A: We turn our heart to the Lord.

P: Let us give thanks to the Lord our God.

A: Truly it is right (to do so).

P: Truly, Lord, it is good
that we give you thanks,
that we glorify you,
you, our God,
you, our Father,
you, the sun we cannot fix our eyes upon,
you, sight itself,
you, the master of all peoples,
you, the master of life,
you, the master of all things,
we give you thanks
through your Son Jesus Christ,
our mediator.

A: Yes, he is our mediator.

P: Holy Father,
we praise you through your Son, Jesus Christ
our mediator.
He is your Word who gives life.
Through him you created heaven and earth; through him you created the streams of the world, the rivers, the ponds, the lakes, and all the fishes that dwell in them. Through him you created the stars, the birds of the sky, the forests, the plains, the savannas, the mountains, and all the animals that dwell therein. Through him you have created all the things that we see, and all that we do not see.

A: Yes, through him, you created all things.

P: You made him master of all things.
You sent him among us that he may become
our Redeemer and Savior.
He is God made human.
By the Holy Spirit,
he took flesh from the Virgin Mary.
We believe it to be so.

A: We believe it to be so.

P: You sent him
that he may gather all men and women
that they may form one single people.
He obeyed,
he died on the cross,
he conquered death,
he rose from the dead.

A: He rose from the dead, he conquered death.

P: This is why
with all the angels,
with all the saints,
with all the dead who are with you, we sing:
You are holy.

A: Holy! Holy! Holy!
Lord, God of the universe,
heaven and earth are filled with your glory.
Hosanna in the highest heavens.
Blessed is he who comes
in the name of the Lord.
Hosanna in the highest heavens.

P: Lord our God, you are holy.
Your only Son, our Lord Jesus Christ, is holy.
Your Spirit, the Paraclete, is holy.
You are holy, almighty God.
We pray you, listen to us.

Look at this bread,
look at this wine,
look at them.
Sanctify them:
May the Holy Spirit descend on these offerings
that we bring before you.
May they become for us the body and blood
of our Lord Jesus Christ.

P: The same night that he was arrested,
he took bread,
He praised you,
he implored you,
he gave you thanks,
he broke the bread
and gave it to his disciples, saying:
Take and eat, all of you, this is my body.
I deliver it for you.
So also, at the end of the meal, he took the cup.
He praised you,
he implored you,
he gave you thanks,
he gave it to his disciples, saying:
Take and drink, all of you, for this is the cup of
my blood, the blood of the new and everlasting
covenant. It will be for you and for all people
the remission of sins.
Do this for my remembrance.

P: It is great, the mystery of faith.

A: You have died.
We believe it.
You have risen.
We believe it.
You will return in glory.
We believe it.

continued on page 46

continued from page 45

P: Lord our God,
we remember the death and resurrection
of your Son.
We offer to you the bread of life.
We offer to you the cup of salvation.
We thank you for making us your chosen ones
worthy to serve in your presence.

Lord God of mercy,
behold, we shall eat the body of Christ;
we shall drink the blood of Christ.
We therefore ask you:
Have mercy on us.
Send your Spirit upon us.
May your Spirit gather us together.
May we become one.

A: Lord, may your Spirit gather us together.
May we become one.

P: Lord, remember your church.
Its presence is felt all over the world.
May all Christians love one another,
as you love us.
Remember the pope. . . .
Remember our bishop. . . .
Remember those who are faithfully guarding
over the apostolic faith.
Remember those who govern the nations.

A: Lord, remember all of them.

P: Lord, remember our brothers (and sisters)
who have died in the hope of resurrection
or of salvation.
Remember them all.
Remember all those who have left this earth,
whose hearts you know.
Remember all of them.
Receive them in your presence.
May they behold your face.

A: Lord, remember all of them.

P: Lord, we pray you,
remember all of us.
May we be received in your presence some day,
where you dwell with the blessed Virgin Mary,
mother of God,
the Apostles and the saints of all ages,
all those whom you love
and who have loved you.
May we then be in your presence
to praise and glorify you
through your Son, Jesus Christ, our Lord.

Presider	All:
Lord, may we glorify your name!	Yes!
Your name!	Yes!
Very honorable!	Yes!
Father!	Yes!
Son!	Yes!
Holy Spirit!	Yes!
May we glorify it!	Yes!
Today!	Yes!
Tomorrow!	Yes!
For ever and ever!	Yes!

Adapted from the translation of Nwaka Chris Egbulem in The Power of Africentric Celebrations: Inspirations from the Zaire Liturgy *(New York: Crossroad, 1996), pp. 141–159. © 1996 Crossroad Publishing. Used with permission. This is taken from the text proposed in 1980, which, Egbulem notes, is closer to what the church in Zaire wanted than the final text approved in 1988.*

in language that the culture finds to be a particularly persuasive way to keep memory. The churches in India and Africa in particular have composed new prayers that draw on images and styles of language that engage local sensibilities.

The variety of local prayers that reflect "the genius and talents of the various races and peoples" (SC, 37–40) enriches the whole church. Such variety is "a genuine treasure; one anaphora complements another."[7]

ECUMENICAL CONVERGENCE

Further testimony to the centrality and essential dynamics of the eucharistic prayer is the unprecedented ecumenical convergence in the celebration of the eucharistic prayer. Reaping the results of scholars' study of the prayer and its history, many churches of the Anglican communion and of the Reformation have recovered the prayer at the altar as a eucharistic prayer, with the move from thanksgiving to supplication. Often, these churches have sought a variety of texts: some fixed prayers, others with variable sections, others more free-form to allow for the retrieval of the tradition of extemporaneous but guided prayer. The Episcopal *Book of Common Prayer* offers four new prayers; the Methodist *At the Lord's Table* collects 22 prayers; the Presbyterian *Service for the Lord's Day* gives eight prayers; and the Lutheran *Book of Worship* contains four.[8]

A stage "in the worldwide recovery of the eucharistic prayer" was reached with the publication of the so-called Lima liturgy by the World Council of Churches. The Faith and Order Statement sets out the meaning of the eucharist for ecumenical reflection:

> The eucharist, which always includes both word and sacrament, is a proclamation and a celebration of the work of God. It is the great thanksgiving to the Father for everything accomplished in creation, redemption and sanctification, for everything accomplished by God now in the church and in the world in spite of the sins of human beings, for everything that God will accomplish in bringing the Kingdom to fulfillment.[10]

The text of a eucharistic prayer along with an order for the celebration of the liturgy was offered in the effort to promote common celebration.

Doctrinal and disciplinary issues continue to be hammered out in dialogues between the Roman Catholic, Anglican, Orthodox and Lutheran churches. These dialogues take on increased importance as we seek that unity of the Body of Christ in light of our common baptism into

Ecumenical Affirmation

The best way towards unity in eucharistic celebration and communion is the renewal of the eucharist itself in the different churches in regard to teaching and liturgy. The churches should test their liturgies in the light of the eucharistic agreement now in the process of attainment.

The liturgical reform movement has brought the churches closer together in the manner of celebrating the Lord's Supper. However, a certain liturgical diversity compatible with our common eucharistic faith is recognized as a healthy and enriching fact. The affirmation of a common eucharistic faith does not imply uniformity in either liturgy or practice.

In the celebration of the eucharist, Christ gathers, teaches and nourishes the church. It is Christ who invites to the meal and who presides at it. He is the shepherd who leads the people of God, the prophet who announces the Word of God, the priest who celebrates the mystery of God. In most churches this presidency is signified by an ordained minister. The one who presides at the eucharistic celebration in the name of Christ makes clear that the rite is not the assemblies' own creation or possession; the eucharist is received as a gift from Christ living in his church. The minister of the eucharist is the ambassador who represents the divine initiative and expresses the connection of the local community with other local communities in the universal church.

Christian faith is deepened by the celebration of the Lord's Supper. Hence the eucharist should be celebrated frequently. Many differences of theology, liturgy, and practice are connected with the varying frequency with which the holy communion is celebrated.

As the eucharist celebrates the resurrection of Christ, it is appropriate that it should take place at least every Sunday. As it is the new sacramental meal of the people of God, every Christian should be encouraged to receive communion frequently. . . .

The increased mutual understanding expressed in the present statement may allow some churches to attain greater measure of eucharistic communion among themselves and so bring closer the day when Christ's divided people will be visibly united around the Lord's table.

Excerpts from Baptism, Eucharist, and Ministry, *Faith and Order Paper 111, pp. 16–17. © 1982 World Council of Churches, Geneva, Switzerland. Used with permission.*

Christ Jesus. The fact that the divided sisters and brothers pray almost identical prayers has tremendous implications for healing divisions.

A Reform Not Yet Grasped

Altogether, we have gained considerable momentum toward a renewed praying of the eucharist: the conciliar reform and developments of the notion of church, the retrieval of the prayer of thanksgiving and supplication as the central prayer of Christians, the growing number of concrete cultural expressions of the dynamic of Christian prayer, and the ecumenical development. All these should further and make more urgent the recovery of eucharistic praying on Sunday.

But why does it seem that these reforms and advances have made little impact? What does it mean to say that the eucharistic prayer is a climactic moment of the celebration? What difference does this recovery of the prayer make to who we are as church gathered around the table of the Body and Blood of Christ?

NOTES

1. *Lumen gentium* [hereafter LG], *Dogmatic Constitution on the Church,* in *Vatican Council II: Constitutions, Decrees, Declarations,* rev. ed., ed. A. Flannery (Northport, N.Y.: Costello, 1996), #9.

2. Joseph A. Komonchak, "The Theology of the Local Church: State of the Question," in *The Multicultural Church: A New Landscape in U.S. Theologies,* ed. W. Cenkner (New York: Paulist, 1996), 37.

3. Komonchak, 37.

4. *Sacrosanctum Concilium, Constitution on the Sacred Liturgy* in Flannery, #7.

5. *Prece eucharistica,* Decree promulgating three new eucharistic prayers, 23 May 1968, in *Documents on the Liturgy 1963–1979* [hereafter DOL] (Collegeville: Liturgical Press, 1982), 241, #1930.

6. *Au cours des derniers mois,* Guidelines to assist catechesis on the anaphoras of the Mass, 2 June 1968. DOL 244, #1954.

7. DOL 244, #1953.

8. For a study of these prayers together with the Roman prayers, see *New Eucharistic Prayers: An Ecumenical Study of their Structure and Development,* ed. Frank C. Senn (New York: Paulist, 1987). See also the collection of texts in *Baptism and Eucharist; Ecumenical Convergence in Celebration,* ed. M Thurian and G. Wainwright (Grand Rapids, Mich.: Eerdmans, 1983), 99–255.

9. *Baptism, Eucharist and Ministry,* Faith and Order Paper No. 111 (Geneva: World Council of Churches, 1982), #3.

THE ELEMENTS OF THE EUCHARISTIC PRAYER: WORD AND RITUAL

When we gather at the Lord's table, we stand and do what is graven in our baptized flesh, what we have inherited from our forebears. Bread and wine in hand, we give thanks and praise to God, remembering Jesus in the power of the Spirit. The *General Instruction of the Roman Missal* (GIRM) names the eucharistic prayer "the center and summit of the entire celebration" (GIRM, 54). In order to grasp how the eucharistic prayer could be the center and summit of a parish's Sunday liturgy, it is first crucial to discern what it means to pray the eucharistic prayer, for we are heirs to both the strengths and weaknesses of eucharistic celebration through the past two millennia.

The eucharistic prayer is the central ritual prayer of the church, a complex of word and action by which the church manifests who and whose we are. It is not just some text the pastor reads in front of the assembly, like the announcements. It is the central ritual prayer of the church and demands to be embodied by the whole assembly. Our entire Christian lives and the sum of our Christian future are at stake in this prayer. And it is only right that we think about what it is that we are doing when we lift up our hearts and give thanks to the Lord our God.

INTERNAL RHYTHM

What it means to pray the eucharistic prayer emerges from the very structure of the eucharistic prayer itself. Recalling our inheritance from the

First Testament and early Jewish prayer, we know that the eucharistic prayer's basic internal unity and dynamic both flow from its being a prayer of thankful remembrance that moves to supplication (see GIRM, 54). As the prayer developed in most Christian communities, this basic dynamic received some elaboration and expansion according to particular needs and cultural patterns. The ten different prayers in the sacramentary all have the same basic continuity of structure and thought.[1]

The eucharistic prayer, like the mystery of faith it proclaims, could be compared to a stained-glass window. The one who observes it "from the outside, without light, sees only lead and pieces of glass"; however, the one who sees it "from the inside, lighted by the sun, seizes all its splendor and perceives the figures it represents."[2] Like a stained-glass window, the eucharistic prayer must be considered as a unified whole in which the various sections are intimately connected and thus must be taken together to appreciate the whole.

We could speak of a *canon* of eucharistic praying, that is, a "rule" or "measure" of what is involved when we pray the eucharistic prayer. We have a canon of ten prayers in the Roman Rite. Each of them shares dynamic and unitive flow, yet each highlights various facets of eucharistic praying. What transpires in the eucharistic prayer?

THE CANON OF PRAYER

The GIRM identifies the following as the elements common to eucharistic prayers in the Roman rite:[3]

- Dialogue
- Thanksgiving
- Acclamation (Sanctus)
- Epiclesis
- Supper — Anamnesis — Offering
- Intercessions
- Final Doxology

Each of these elements is an elaboration on, or a particular focus of, the whole move from thanksgiving to supplication.

DIALOGUE While most of the other prayers in the liturgy begin with a simple "Let us pray" or a short expansion on it, the opening of the central prayer is quite formal. This dialogue is also one of the oldest elements of the prayer. It opens the prayer as a whole and indicates what it is that the assembled church is about to do.

The initial exchange—"The Lord be with you/And also with you"—affirms that we are all gathered in Christ. It affirms the unity of the Body of Christ rooted in the Spirit.

Then comes the call: "Lift up your hearts/We lift them up to the Lord." Our "hearts" here stands for our very being; we lift up our entire being to God. All of our joys and tears, our struggles and gains, our hopes and grief, our praise and need—these we lift up, and they are taken into glory. To speak of lifting up our very being indicates the passage to the Father through Jesus in the Spirit that we make in the prayer. It reminds us that the eucharist we make together is possible only because Jesus is now the "one who is seated at the right hand of the throne of the Majesty in the heavens" (Hebrews 8:1). Our liturgy, our eucharist, is taken up in the prayer of Jesus to the Father. Jesus draws all members of the Body to the Father and brings them life by the Spirit.[4] "When we hear this *ultimate* summons, let us ask ourselves: Are our hearts turned to the Lord, is the ultimate treasure of our heart in God?"[5]

The third call resounds: "Let us give thanks to the Lord our God/ It is right to give our thanks and praise." This ancient call and response makes explicit the assembly's action. "The act of thanksgiving is shown thereby to be based on reflection and deliberation; it is an act that is consciously done and involves the whole person."[6]

The ritual dialogue between the presider and the assembly manifests that the whole church makes the eucharist. By engaging in the dialogue, the assembly—led by the presider—manifests how self-evident and becoming the action of the gathered assembly is.[7] It demonstrates the relationship of the presiding minister and the assembly, an ordered gathering with distinctive roles. There is no opposition between the presbyter and the assembly; how could there be among the baptized? Yet as the assembly's presiding minister, the presbyter is its voice in prayer to God.

The assembly announces its public work and endorses the presidential ministry of the presbyter, without whose presidential activity we would not have an assembly at all. The presider "is not simply one member among others, but an essential member whom the very nature of the assembly requires."[8]

THANKSGIVING In most of the current prayers of the Roman Rite, the thanksgiving of the eucharistic prayer is concentrated in its first section, the *preface,* or "proclamation." The more than 85 prefaces all display a similar pattern. First, their stylized beginnings link them up with the call to thanksgiving and assert that it is through Jesus Christ our Lord that we give thanks. The prefaces then focus on some particular aspect of what God has done in Jesus for our salvation; this often is connected with the feast or liturgical season. Even feasts of Mary and the saints relate the celebration to what God has done in Christ Jesus. We see in this specific naming that "we do not give thanks on our own initiative, rather, we are urged to it by our experience of having found favor with God in Christ."[9]

And what a mighty God whose awesome deeds we remember in thanksgiving! The "God we cannot see" sent his only Son, "the one begotten before all ages" who "appeared in human form." It is Jesus, who came "to raise the fallen world, to make creation whole again, and to lead humanity from exile back to God" (Christmas II). By Jesus' suffering on the cross, "he freed us from unending death; by rising from the dead, he gave us eternal life" (Ordinary Time II); "for his death is our ransom from death, and in his resurrection all are raised to new life" (Easter II). We gather as God's holy people, the church, to remember and to give thanks. And we ask God to be with us once more as we "watch for the day when Christ will come again in majesty and glory" (Advent I), when God will be all in all.

HOLY, HOLY, HOLY For all that God has done for us in Christ Jesus, we cannot help but cry, "Holy!" So caught up in the love of God, who has done so much for us, we thunder forth with praise to God. Naming and celebrating our life in Christ made possible by God's grace, we move in song before the very throne of God, for in our praise and thanksgiving we are lifted up through Christ to the Father. Our song not only shakes the walls of our church building but echoes in the halls of heaven. We, like the angels, move before God, aflame with love:

> Angels, I read, belong to nine different orders. Seraphs are the highest; they are aflame with love for God, and stand closer to him than the others. Seraphs love God. . . . The seraphs are born of a stream of fire issuing from under God's throne. They are, according to Dionysius the Areopagite, "all wings," having, as Isaiah notes, six wings apiece, two of which they fold over their eyes. Moving perpetually toward God, they perpetually praise him, crying "Holy, Holy, Holy. . . . But according to some rabbinic writings, they can sing only the first "Holy" before the intensity of their love ignites them and dissolves them again, perpetually, into flames.[10]

General Instruction of the Roman Missal

54. Now the center and summit of the entire celebration begins: the eucharistic prayer, a prayer of thanksgiving and sanctification. The priest invites the people to lift up their hearts to the Lord in prayer and thanks; he unites them with himself in the prayer he addresses in their name to the Father through Jesus Christ. The meaning of the prayer is that the entire congregation joins itself to Christ in acknowledging the great things God has done and in offering the sacrifice.

55. The chief elements making up the eucharistic prayer are these:

a. Thanksgiving (expressed especially in the preface): In the name of the entire people of God, the priest praises the Father and gives thanks to him for the whole work of salva-

tion or for some special aspect of it that corresponds to the day, feast, or season.

b. Acclamation: joining with the angels, the congregation sings or recites the Sanctus. This acclamation is an intrinsic part of the eucharistic prayer and all the people join with the priest in singing or reciting it.

c. Epiclesis: in special invocations the church calls on God's power and asks that the gifts offered by human hands be consecrated, that is, become Christ's body and blood, and that the victim to be received in communion be the source of salvation for those who will partake.

d. Institution narrative and consecration: In the words and actions of Christ, that sacrifice is celebrated which he himself instituted at the Last Supper, when, under the

Our thrice-holy hymn embraces earth and heaven. All things seen and unseen—all reality—becomes caught up in thanksgiving. Like Isaiah, we glimpse the eternal glory of God, at whose right hand Christ now stands. And Jesus is able "for all time to save those who approach God through him, since he always lives to make intercession for them" (Hebrews 7:25).

Following the Sanctus, a transition takes place as the prayer moves from thanksgiving to supplication that God act once more. In Eucharistic Prayers I and II (hereafter abbreviated EP I, EP II, and so on) and Reconciliation I, it is a very short transition that echoes the Sanctus. In EP III and Reconciliation II, it is a bit longer; in EP IV, the Sanctus itself is a transition to an extended section of thanksgiving that remembers the scope of salvation wrought by God in Christ.

appearances of bread and wine, he offered his body and blood, gave them to his apostles to eat and drink, then commanded that they carry on this mystery.

e. Anamnesis: In fulfillment of the command received from Christ through the apostles, the church keeps his memorial by recalling especially his passion, resurrection and ascension.

f. Offering: in this memorial, the church—and in particular the church here and now assembled—offers the spotless victim to the Father in the Holy Spirit. The church's intention is that the faithful not only offer this victim but also learn to offer themselves and so to surrender themselves, through Christ the Mediator, to an ever more complete union with the Father and with each other, so that at last God may be all in all.

g. Intercessions: The intercessions make it clear that the eucharist is celebrated in communion with the entire church of heaven and earth and that the offering is made for the church and all its members, living and dead, who are called to share in the salvation and redemption purchased by Christ's body and blood.

h. Final doxology: the praise of God is expressed in the doxology, to which the people's acclamation is an assent and a conclusion. The eucharistic prayer calls for all to listen in silent reverence, but also to take part through the acclamations for which the rite makes provision.

Excerpts from the English translation of the General Instruction of the Roman Missal *from* Documents on the Liturgy, 1963–1979: Conciliar, Papal and Curial Texts. © *1982, International Committee on English in the Liturgy, Inc. All rights reserved. Used with permission.*

Epiclesis The next two movements of the eucharistic prayer form the hinges on which the whole of it turns—the epiclesis and the supper narrative-anamnesis. Past ways and narrow vision have led us to isolate one or another from the whole movement of the prayer, but neither can be grasped without seeing the eucharistic prayer as a whole.[11]

The Eucharistic Epiclesis

As long as one remains conscious of the basic dependence of the community upon God for the realization of the eucharist, as long as one keeps in mind that the assembly always stands before God as a praying assembly, there is little danger of ignoring God's absolute sovereignty in one's understanding of the Eucharist. One of the greatest values of an epiclesis proper lies in its ability to underscore the fact that the believing assembly must pray for the realization of the eucharist.

The fully developed epiclesis, whatever else it may be, is always a prayer. Even the view that the primitive meaning of "epiclesis" was the naming of a name must include this prayer aspect or face the accusation of magical tendencies.

In the epiclesis the assembly, having recalled the events of saving history and having made grateful acknowledgment of these events, confesses its own helplessness. It appeals to God to act upon the bread and wine in view of those about to partake of them. In other words, the assembly appeals to God to transform both the gifts and the assembled faithful so that this celebration of the Eucharist may bring about a mutual eucharistic presence. The assembly asks God to intervene here and now so that this cele-

bration may express and deepen the unity between Christ and the faithful and the unity of the faithful with each other and with the Father in Christ. All of this it asks for through the action of the Holy Spirit. How and when this action is to take place is God's concern. The believing community's concern is to partake of the gifts with the firm assurance, springing from faith, that God has answered its prayer. One major contribution of the epiclesis proper to a healthy understanding of the eucharist lies precisely in its ability to express the helplessness and dependence and, at the same time, the prayerful confidence of the assembly.

Thus, the epiclesis serves various functions. It can bring out the fact that God realizes the eucharist *for* the assembly and that God does so *through* the whole assembly. It can also bring out the fact that this assembly is a praying assembly, totally dependent upon God for the initiative in realizing the eucharistic encounter. It is a question not of exclusivity but of complementarity, and an epiclesis proper is well suited to voice these various facets simultaneously.

Excerpted from J.H. McKenna, "Eucharistic Epiclesis: Myopia or Microcosm?" Theological Studies 36:2 (June 1975): 273–274. © 1975 Theological Studies, Inc. Used with permission.

The word *epiclesis* means "calling down upon" or "invocation." The eucharistic prayer moves into supplication. The epiclesis, which in our current prayers has two parts, is the "why" of our eucharistic praying. The first part of the epiclesis asks God "to send down" or "to send forth" the Holy Spirit or to "sanctify" the gifts by the "power of the Holy Spirit." What we ask here is that our gifts of bread and wine be transformed into the Body and Blood of Christ. The second part of the epiclesis is the very reason for the first part: It asks that we who partake of the Body and Blood of Christ be transformed by the Spirit to be built up further as that Body of Christ in the world, that we partake of all the blessings of the cross that we have asked God to remember. And so we pray in EP II:

> Send down your Spirit upon these gifts to make them holy,
> that they may become for us the body and blood of our Lord,
> Jesus Christ.

> We pray that all of us who share in the body and blood of
> Christ may be gathered into one by the Holy Spirit.

We ask that the gifts be transformed in order that we who share them might be transformed. And we invoke the Spirit because the "Spirit brings us into the reality that is the body of Christ."[12] We, a people drenched by Spirit-filled waters, glistening from a Spirit-filled unction, stirred by a Spirit-filled story, call upon the very Spirit of God who wrenched Jesus from the jaws of death. We invoke the Holy Spirit over our gifts of bread and wine and over ourselves. Calling down the Spirit, we plead with God to continue to be in our midst and transform us in a communion pledged and shared in the banquet of the Body and Blood of Christ.

SUPPER NARRATIVE – ANAMNESIS – OFFERING The word *anamnesis* refers to the memorial prayer that follows the Last Supper narrative and the memorial acclamation. We are confident to make that plea because we are moved by our memorial thanksgiving. And in the eucharistic prayer, our memory of God's decisive action for us culminates in the memory of the pasch of Jesus, which is summed up in the account of the Last Supper. Jesus commanded, "Do this in memory of me." And the Last Supper narrative and the memorial prayer following it tell what the church does by reason of that command: We keep the memory of Jesus by taking up bread and wine and accepting Jesus' sacrificial attitude. The bread and wine "are the concrete embodiment and synthesis of the memorial" of Christ's pasch.[13]

We have examined how the Last Supper, because it was a prophetic word and act, is a synthesis of the mystery of salvation that God wrought in Jesus. The Last Supper narrative is addressed to God as prayer. It is a proclamation, not a dramatization. It proclaims the ultimate object of our memorial thanksgiving: the mystery of Jesus accomplished in the pasch. The words of the supper narrative are not a direct quote from any of the gospels. Rather, the recital of these words is the ritual remembering by the church; it is part of our thanksgiving prayer and supplication to God through words culled from tradition and shaped into prayer.

When the presider recounts the words of Christ in the Last Supper narrative, the presider is not Jesus speaking to the disciples in the upper room. The presider is, and remains, the ordained minister of the church here gathered who continues to speak to God in prayer. Yet the words of Christ, though he spoke them in the unrepeatable event of the supper, were directed to our then far-off future. In our gathering here and now to remember that event, the presider, praying with the words ascribed to Jesus, proclaims those words in eucharistic prayer. They are certainly the words of Christ, because they are the words of the Body of the risen Christ at prayer. But they are not immediately in Christ's mouth; rather, they are on the mouth of the church, whose voice is gathered into one by the ordained minister.[14]

The Last Supper narrative not only proclaims the very center of our memorial thanksgiving, the pasch, but the words are prayed in the context of having asked God to sanctify our gifts by the Spirit. In our asking God to remember in the supper narrative, we are asking God to act in fidelity to the new covenant established in Jesus' blood through the Holy Spirit, who draws us to the Father through Christ.

Once more we pray Christ's command to remember him: "Do this in memory of me." And so in the memorial prayer that is intimately linked to the supper narrative, we state exactly that we are obedient to the command of Christ to remember him. In the memorial prayer, we sum up what it is that we as church do:

> Remembering therefore his death and resurrection, we offer you, Lord God, this life-giving bread, this saving cup. EP II

> Calling to mind [therefore], Lord God, the death your Son endured for our salvation, his glorious resurrection and ascension into heaven and eagerly awaiting the day of his return, we offer you in thanksgiving this holy and living sacrifice. EP III

> And so, Lord God, we celebrate the memorial of our redemption. EP IV

Jesus said, "Do this." The church says, "Therefore, Lord God, we do remember Jesus." In the memorial prayer, we point to our eucharist "as the fulfillment and presence of the divine blessings given to humanity in Jesus Christ who is remembered."[15] And we acknowledge that the same Jesus is present by the Holy Spirit to us and to all humanity.

The memorial acclamation that we sing between the supper narrative and the memorial prayer acclaims Jesus, whose memorial command we keep. The singing of the memorial acclamation by the assembly forms an integral part of the prayer by which the assembly manifests its participation in the memorial thanksgiving, the expression of its obedience to Christ, and proclaims the paschal joy of life in the risen Christ, who will come again in glory. In other translations of the *Roman Missal* and anticipated in the revisions of the *Sacramentary* for the United States, the bidding by presider or deacon (whose role of bidding the assembly during prayer is well attested) cues the assembly's intervention and shows that it is integrated into the flow of the prayer:

> A
> Great is the mystery of faith!

> Christ has died,
> Christ is risen,
> Christ will come again.

B
Praise to you, Lord Jesus.

Dying you destroyed our death,
rising you restored our life.
Lord Jesus, come in glory.

C
Christ is the bread of life.

When we eat this bread and drink this cup,
we proclaim your death, Lord Jesus,
until you come in glory.

D
Jesus Christ is Lord.

Lord, by your cross and resurrection
you have set us free.
You are the Savior of the world.

The eucharistic prayer itself is always addressed to the Father through Christ in the Spirit. The acclamations of the assembly in the prayer are generally addressed to Christ. This distinction makes clear that the memorial of the presider and assembly together manifest the whole movement of the prayer.[16] These acclamations are different from hymns, psalms or litanic refrains; they are bound to the prayer and are "shouts of joy which arise from the whole assembly as forceful and meaningful assents to God's word and action."[17] These acclamations emphasize the thanksgiving character of the prayer and give a summation to the memorial of the pasch. Part of the fabric of the prayer, the acclamation should also lead to the supplication that flows from the memorial thanksgiving.[18]

INTERCESSIONS This memory of Christ, risen from the snares of death, instills hope in us that God's embrace of love is stronger even than death and will not let us go. The resurrection promises not only future life but life here and now. This memory of Christ trampling death offers us the hope of being transformed and tethered in communion by the Spirit. Confident that God is faithful to the covenant promise, we ask God to send the Spirit to unite us by our sharing in the Body and Blood of Christ given for the remission of sins.

In our memorial thanksgiving, we pass with Christ to the Father in the Spirit. We, as the Body of Christ, empty ourselves in our prayer of thanks and give ourselves in love to God out of obedience to Jesus' command. And as the Father was well pleased, as the Father embraced the Son even in death and poured out the Spirit of love by raising Christ from the dead, so we, too, as the Body of Christ before God, trust in God's steadfast love and mercy and ask that God once more pour out the Spirit on us.

Nothing that the Spirit touches remains the same. And so we, bolstered by the Spirit, ask God to remember our church, our world, those who have gone before us. We pray in communion with Mary and the saints and with our own dead. The memory of Christ's pasch, of life in the midst of suffering and death, moves us to "remember a future that is still outstanding."[19] The intercessions remind us "of the 'not yet' dimension of Christian life in this world at the very moment in which the eschatological 'now' of the real presence of Christ is celebrated and experienced."[20] The pledge of life despite death is our sharing of the eucharist. Our communion at the altar-table is indeed the "communion of saints," the saints gathered on earth sharing the holy food as did the saints gone before us.

FINAL DOXOLOGY AND GREAT AMEN The whole prayer of doxology, of praise and thanksgiving, swells to a final rush of praise:

> Through [Christ our Lord], with him, and in him,
> in the unity of the Holy Spirit,
> all glory and honor is yours almighty Father,
> forever and ever.
> Amen.

The final doxology proclaims once more the whole movement of our prayer to the Father, through, with and in Jesus, which is all possible because of the communion of the Holy Spirit. It is the climax of the whole "sanctificatory movement . . . since the divine name is formally proclaimed in its fullest and most explicit form."[21] The assembly's "Amen," the most ancient of all acclamations, is the most important acclamation we sing. It affirms that all that has been proclaimed is indeed right and just, that it is truly the thanks and praise of the church. Such an Amen surges from the depths of our body, the depths of our soul. It surges from the church, this assembly. Our prayer, given voice by the leader of our assembly, is sealed. Yes, what has been said and done at this table is the truth about God and the world. The work of the Amen is not to end the prayer. In fact, this Amen "calls us into the future" that the prayer opens before us.[22]

Center and Summit

When we pray the eucharistic prayer, we manifest who we are: the Spirit-filled Body of Christ. The eucharistic prayer manifests the core of baptized life and what a Christian community looks, sounds and feels like. Here God and the church work the ongoing transformation of those who open themselves to the Spirit. In the eucharistic prayer, we present ourselves in faith to God as "a living sacrifice, holy and acceptable to God," our spiritual worship (Romans 12:1). Any other notion of the eucharistic prayer — for example, that it is what the priest does so that we can "get communion" — is sadly lacking.

God has called us to be church, the Body of Christ in the world. In the eucharistic prayer and in communion, we are united with Christ, emptying ourselves in praise and thanksgiving to the Father. Christ the head is united with his Body, the church, and the Father pours out the Spirit in love. In the sacramental communion, we are transformed and pledge ourselves to be broken and poured out in the world. In the eucharistic prayer we are obedient to the command of Jesus to keep the memory of his pasch: taking, blessing, breaking, giving. This is the summit of our vocation as baptized, priestly people.

WHICH TO PRAY?

How do we measure up to the rule of eucharistic praying set out by the liturgical books? Does the local assembly make deliberate and careful selection of the texts available each week? Or does this remain the last-minute page flip of the presider based on personal taste or some perception of time constraints?

The eucharistic prayer is the church's prayer. If this eucharistic praying is the center and summit, if it is the manifestation of the church, the choice of text must be deliberate and thoughtful. There are ten eucharistic prayers approved for use in the United States. After at least two decades of use, have we discovered their strengths and their weaknesses? Only two, EP II and EP III, are used with great frequency. The revisers of the Missal intended to provide more variety and allow the multiplicity of texts to make up for the limitations of any one in particular. Is all this diversity a good thing? Are EP II and EP III chosen so often because of their length or their quality? What principles for choosing have emerged in these last two decades? What follows is a brief look at each prayer.

EUCHARISTIC PRAYER I Also known as the Roman Canon, this prayer is the theological, liturgical and spiritual legacy of Latin church and has remained much the same since the seventh century. For centuries it was the single eucharistic prayer of the Roman church. It was the sign of communion with the church of Rome, and it witnesses to the apostolicity of the faith. It allows for a variable section of thanksgiving, and on certain feasts the celebration of the day is mentioned in parts of the petitions of the prayer. But it remains a daunting text to pray. The legal and cultic language, the style and cadence, the imagery and expression no longer move the hearts of the modern parish. It is more likely to be perceived as mystifying rather than as evocative of mystery, more imposing than majestic. The lists of saints is often truncated, usually cutting out the women saints. Perhaps this prayer would be best prayed on apostles' feasts or on feasts of saints or of the dedications of churches. Finally, this prayer makes no mention of the Holy Spirit, and that is cause for deep concern.

Eucharistic Prayer II Inspired by an ancient prayer, EP II is intended for weekdays, small assemblies and Masses with children. Its preface is intended to be used with it, but the body of EP II can be used with other prefaces. Its brevity and style have made it quite popular. It also has interpolations for Sundays throughout the year and for celebrations of the sacraments and other rites. Time must never be a factor when selecting the eucharistic prayer; the degree of solemnity of the day and the season of the year should be the factors. Even so, EP II is probably often chosen because it is short; happily, it is also a powerful text.

Eucharistic Prayer III This prayer was crafted to be used on Sundays with the preface of the season or feast. It provides insertions, also called *embolisms*, for feasts and for the celebration of the rites and sacraments. It has a slightly expanded section of thanksgiving after the Sanctus that prolongs the thanksgiving themes of the preface before moving to supplication. This prayer is a good choice for Sundays in the Christmas and Easter seasons and on other major feasts.

Eucharistic Prayer IV Unlike the first three eucharistic prayers, the fourth eucharistic prayer has an unchangeable preface. "It presents in an orderly and somewhat developed way, a complete synthesis of the history of salvation. . . . This requires the preface to be limited to the themes of creation in general and the creation of angels, the first two stages in the history of salvation."[23] To change the preface to a seasonal one would be to the detriment of the prayer's style of memorial thanksgiving. This prayer is most clearly trinitarian in its movement. The preface praises God, the Creator. After the Holy, Holy, it recalls what God has done through Jesus and then moves to invocation of the Spirit. This prayer is often neglected because it is long—but in reality, it is only a few minutes longer than the others. The orderly recall of God's great deeds can be of tremendous importance pastorally. When done well, this prayer jogs memories and begins to engage us in a fuller style of eucharistic praying. EP IV might well alternate with EP III in Ordinary Time.

Eucharistic Prayer for Masses of Reconciliation I and II These two prayers, originally drafted in 1974 and intended for use during the Holy

Year of 1975, have become part of the Roman repertoire of eucharistic prayers. They are cited as especially appropriate for "special celebrations with a theme of reconciliation and penance, especially during Lent and on the occasion of pilgrimage or spiritual meetings."[24] These prayers are rather unique with regard to the Roman church's emphasis on seasonal or occasional variability. These prayers take reconciliation in Christ through the paschal mystery as the "theme" to motivate thanksgiving. They are composed around that theme from preface to final intercessions; therefore, they should not be used with a variable or seasonal preface.

These prayers seem most suitable for the season of Lent, except in year A, when the prefaces directly related to the readings can be used. They might also find a place in a parish's repertoire on some Sundays during Ordinary Time.

EUCHARISTIC PRAYERS FOR MASSES WITH CHILDREN I, II AND III These three eucharistic prayers have limited use. They are for assemblies of children who have not yet reached the age of preadolescence.[25] They are intended to draw children into the way of eucharistic praying in order to lead them back to the Sunday adult assembly, where they will eventually assume a fuller role. Prayer I is for children who have just been introduced to the eucharist; prayers II and III are for children who have more awareness of and greater experience with the eucharistic celebration. The prayers themselves are very flexible and adaptable to circumstances, which is perhaps their greatest strength. The prayers are distinctively composed in a dialogical style and make use of more frequent acclamations and some "pedagogical" changes in structure. Except for the third prayer (which allows for a variable preface in the paschal season), they are through-composed and do not support the variable prefaces.

These prayers are infrequently used. One reason may be that, more than the other prayers, they make it clear that good music for acclamations is a necessity. That aside, the prayers pose many questions. They differ in style and content from the eucharistic prayers that children will pray in the adult assembly; does good use of these prayers foster an active participation that the children will not be able to exercise later? "The style and experience of liturgy that the children celebrate every Sunday with their parents and friends is not what they encounter at special peri-odic children's Masses. As a result . . . the children's Masses can become more an exercise in performance rather than an expression of the faith of children that leads them back to the Sunday assembly."[26] Perhaps the Consilium's intention that EP II be used for Masses with children makes more sense, but it requires careful catechesis.

While these prayers for Masses with children are not to be used for assemblies with adults, many adult assemblies have looked to the *children's* prayers for a model of eucharistic praying that incorporates more acclamation and dialogue. Is there an aspect of the canon of praying in the children's prayers — with their emphasis on acclamation — that can extend the assembly's own repertoire?

EUCHARISTIC PRAYER FOR MASSES FOR VARIOUS NEEDS AND OCCASIONS

Sunday is not one of the occasions where this prayer would be used. The decree and introduction to the prayer explicitly state: "The use of this text . . . will follow the norms established in this typical edition, so that the text of the prayer may be used in harmony with the formularies of the Masses for Various Needs and Occasions." What seems to be at issue here is the Roman predilection for the variable preface that corresponds to the Sunday or feast being celebrated.

The way this prayer is set out can be confusing. First, this prayer originated with the synod of Swiss bishops in 1972 and was approved for use in Switzerland in 1974. Subsequently, the other countries of Europe adopted it. The prayer, like the reconciliation prayers, is composed around a theme that is the motive for thanksgiving: God leads the church to unity in Christ, who is the way, the truth, and the life.[27] The invariable part of the prayer focuses on this theme, while the variable preface and — unprecedented for Roman liturgy — a variable intercession section pick up the theme's different aspects. "There is, thus, a close unity between the invariable part and the variable parts, so much so that the variable parts [four prefaces with corresponding intercessions] prove to be but four dif-ferent ways of formulating the one theme."[28] Because of this unity, other prefaces are excluded. The theme fits quite well with a church in synod: unity, the way to truth, Christ the guide. The prayer also has a certain quality of language that many find more engaging than the other eucharistic prayers.[29]

The desire of many assemblies to make more frequent use of this prayer, along with the musical setting provided and the additional acclamations, seems to suggest that the need and the occasion for the prayer might be greater than envisioned. Those making choices here must recognize the reason for the restricted use of this eucharistic prayer: the weight that the Roman church puts on the memorial thanksgiving of God's saving work in the life and death of Christ, unfolded over the course of the liturgical cycle. The place where we name those events is the preface, and this eucharistic prayer excludes a preface directly linked to the Sunday, season or feast.

PREFACES Considerable care should go into the selection of the preface for the Sunday celebration. Again, a preface is chosen to resonate with the whole of the church's prayer and situation on that Sunday. What are the scripture readings for the Sunday in question? Do any of the prefaces echo the readings so as to reinforce our identity as a community of memory and thanksgiving? What is happening in our assemblies? Is there need for memory of who we are as a priestly people? of forgiveness? of God's unfailing love? of Jesus' triumph? of the Spirit's work? of future promise? The starting point, as we saw, for all memory is what is happening in the here and now.

WHAT DIFFERENCE DOES IT MAKE?

Do we realize the power of these prayers when absorbed over time? After all, we are striving to be "living sacrifices of praise" and thanksgiving, which demands that our living be molded by our praying. Will a parish that has a steady diet of EP II act, sound and pray differently than a parish that regularly uses EP IV? Will a parish that prays EP IV be more apt to perceive its ministry for justice in Jesus' liberating activity — proclaiming good news to the poor and release to prisoners? Will those who pray EP II need to be reminded in the homily of the scope and images of God's covenant relationship with our human kind (because this is absent from the text of EP II)? Will a parish that uses EP I to the regular exclusion of the other prayers have little sensibility for the role of the Holy Spirit in our transformation but a keen sense of the communion of saints? Will parishes that pray the reconciliation prayers come to put their ministry in the perspective of "the one eternal banquet" where all people will be gathered and the fullness of peace shall reign?

Careful selection of the eucharistic prayer throughout the liturgical cycle can support the continuing efforts of our Sunday assemblies to pray it. Assemblies will become aware of the richness and variety of texts and of the texts' power to shape them. In order to develop strong and regular patterns, a parish team could prepare a scheme that sets out which prayer will be used in which season. For Ordinary Time, blocks of Sundays long enough to ensure familiarity with and attention to the text could be established. The parish plan would be followed at all the parish Masses.

The choice of which text for the eucharistic prayer, and which text for the preface (when the prayer allows a choice), is extremely important. But the right choice of a good text is only a bare beginning. The best texts are lifeless without worthy proclamation and, even more, without the ritual habits that involve the assembly in full, conscious and active participation in the eucharistic prayer.

Beyond Speech: Dimensions of Ritual Performance

Eucharistic praying is not just a matter of the words we use but what we do when we are praying them. We are in the domain of ritual and must attend to the space, objects, time, sounds and actions.[30] We saw that even when the same prayer was prayed over the course of a millennium, the way it was prayed — as much or more than the text itself — shaped and expressed what the prevailing understanding of eucharistic praying was.

The ritual enactment of the prayer and the ritual context of the prayer have tremendous impact on what meanings, beliefs, memories, hopes, values and relationships are articulated.[31] If the eucharistic prayer is the center and summit of the entire celebration, then the ritual context must bespeak its centrality. Attention to the nonverbal is crucial if one

Eucharistic praying is not just a matter of the words we use but what we do while we are praying them. We are in the domain of ritual and must attend to the space, objects, time, sounds and actions.

realizes that the nonverbal negotiates and hands on meaning more subtly than the text itself.

The question of how a parish prays the eucharistic prayer, then, is not a matter of local idiosyncrasy or the presider's whimsy. The eucharistic prayer is the church's prayer that demands to be embodied by the local assembly.

The sacramentary sets out certain directives that serve to guide the celebration in an orderly way and foster a common rhythm. These directives tell us that liturgy requires a careful choreography and style. These directives need also to be read through the lens of the needs of the local community. In a phrase that still bears repeating, "Good celebrations foster and nourish faith. Poor celebrations may weaken and destroy it."[32]

Attention to detail is demanded by the integrity of the assembly and its liturgy. To be concerned about the details of careful liturgical celebration is not slavish adherence to "rubrics." The directives ask more of us: They ask that we embody the spirit through the letter of the law. Slipshod celebrations spurn the church at prayer and sunder the limbs from the Body, handing stones to those who ask for bread. Moreover, we need to bear in mind that tradition does not only entail what has been handed on to us. In and through our celebration we are actively handing on what we have received and are shaping the next generation of our parish. Doing it well promises life; doing it poorly ensures demise.

SPACE The architectural frame of the liturgy has a profound effect on our eucharistic praying. Consider the following three floor plans:

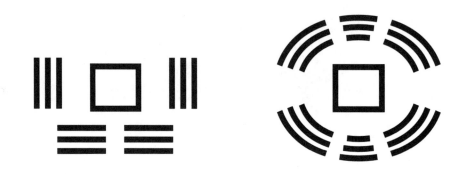

The Elements of the Eucharistic Prayer: Word and Ritual

How can these spaces be shaped into places where the ordered liturgical assembly can pray?[33] If the assembly is small, how might it actually gather around the table in any of these three? If the number in the assembly precludes its gathering around the table, how might each floor plan best accommodate at least some members of the assembly gathering around the table? Is there an altar rail that blocks access to the altar-table? Why is it there? To have the assembly physically gather around the table—around it, not just in front of it—seems to be more than just an image of praying the eucharistic prayer together. It might be, rather, a prerequisite that every parish should strive to fulfill in its long-term planning. Trapped in pews and physically removed from the table, we will never reclaim what it means to pray the eucharistic prayer:

> Pews distance the congregation, disenfranchise the faithful and rend the assembly. Filling a church with immovable pews is similar to placing bleachers directly on a basketball court: It not only interferes with movement but changes the event into something entirely different.[34]

It has become a practice in many parishes to use higher- or lower-intensity lighting over sections of the worship space during the liturgy. For example, the ambo is spotlighted during the liturgy of the word while the table is under dim light, and then this is reversed for the liturgy of the eucharist. There is an inherent danger, though, in this "cue lighting" borrowed from the world of theater. Basically, the assembly is never a passive spectator and should never be cast as such by dim lighting at any time. The altar, ambo and font are the central symbols of the liturgical space. In fact, from the very entrance procession, the altar is reverenced. Lighting can be of value in our visual culture, but we must remember that liturgy is not something we watch. Liturgy is action. The attention is not on the person or place of reading but on the act of proclaiming and celebrating the word of God. The attention is not on the altar or on the minister there but on the act of the whole assembly, formed by the word, who now give thanks and eat and drink.

OBJECTS The eucharistic prayer is prayed over the gifts of bread and wine placed on the altar. Despite clear directives over the years (e.g., *This Holy and Living Sacrifice*, by the U.S. Bishops Committee on the Liturgy), we still need to be reminded that only one plate, one cup and one flagon large enough to hold the wine for the communion of the assembly should be on the table.[35] Our large assemblies may call for more flagons of wine, but can we not find plates that can accommodate a number of loaves of bread?

What does the altar itself which we gather around look like? The altar table is named "the central point of the whole eucharistic liturgy" (GIRM, 49). What is it covered with? Do we assure the noble beauty of the cloth and its color, or do we thoughtlessly throw a polyester patchwork of cute sew-ons over the table? Do we still use chalices with thimble-size bowls and corporals the size of a handkerchief? What is the assembly to think if the book of its prayer, the sacramentary, is tattered and worn? We offer bread and wine to God on the table, not eyeglasses, candlesticks, music programs or hymnals. Is it wise to place candles on the altar rather than around it? Would it not be most appropriate to place flowers around or near the table, not on it or in front of it in a way that calls more attention to them than to the table?

The provision made for the incensation of the eucharistic elements during the supper narrative is problematic.[36] A remnant of medieval ceremonial that placed dramatic emphasis on the visual adoration of the eucharistic elements, the incensation at the supper narrative marks a change in the ritual strategies. The whole eucharistic prayer is a prayer of thanksgiving and sanctification. The whole of the prayer is "consecratory." The eucharistic prayer is not about adoration or veneration. It is about doxology. To use incense at the supper narrative speaks one ritual language while the church at prayer is speaking another. A continually burning bowl of incense — our prayer rising before the throne of grace — or a minister swinging a censer back and forth through the entire prayer would be more acceptable options if incense were to be used at all during the prayer.

TIME How is the eucharistic prayer marked in the course of ritual time? If it is the center and summit, the time given to it must be of central concern. This is not simply a question of the amount of time but a question of

The Elements of the Eucharistic Prayer: Word and Ritual

the quality of that time, the ebb and flow within that time. Ritual time is only in part duration; it also includes the way time is punctuated. If the occasion demands lengthy preaching, it certainly may demand lengthy eucharistic praying! The center and summit of the liturgy should be marked in a ritual way. It should become part of a parish's ritual repertory to observe a period of silence before the eucharistic prayer and at its conclusion, perhaps accompanied by a profound inclination. More will be said on the tempo of the prayer when discussing the presider's role.

SOUNDS Though all our senses can be involved in eucharistic praying, speech does hold a kind of primacy. This is to say that the emphasis falls on the oral and the aural, not on the visual and the manual. The eucharistic prayer by its nature demands sung performance.[37] As the Pastoral Introduction states, "Since the eucharistic prayer is the summit of the Mass, its solemn nature and importance are enhanced when it is sung." The principle of progressive solemnity can guide a parish, but the solemnity of every Sunday should be taken seriously.[38]

Not every parish has presiders with musical skill, but the nature of the eucharistic prayer pleads that every effort be made to work toward sung performance. Some argue that we as a people do not remember our story or seek divine intervention in song, that the eucharistic prayer really should not be sung because we talk to each other. Scan through any city or county's radio stations: There is no instance where what matters to the human heart is not taken into song, whether it be country, rap, blues, soul, jazz, hip-hop, pop or rock. We take both what is life-giving and life-threatening into song.

What about the sounds of the words themselves, whether sung or recited? Ritual language is different from ordinary speech and language. While the words we use in ritual may resonate with words we know from everyday speech, ritual involves a rupture with the everyday in such a way that the words we use are formalized, highly stylized, repeated, chanted, poetic. The words of our eucharistic prayer become our privileged words before God.

We need also to be attentive to the extraneous sounds that undermine what our eucharistic praying is about. The GIRM indicates that a server *may* ring a bell "as a signal to the faithful" at the supper narrative and the showing of the host and chalice (109). This is another remnant of the medieval era, when the prayer was unintelligible, shrouded in silence and understood in a dramatic fashion. The ringing of a bell undermines the unity of the eucharistic prayer, places emphasis on the secondary act of showing the elements and suggests to the assembly that it needs to be attentive only at certain moments.

ACTIONS The human body as it occupies and moves in space communicates as much as — sometimes even more than — words. Do the actions we engage in enhance the quality of the prayer or hinder our communal celebration? The sacramentary gives directives for many gestures by the presider, but not by the assembly. What action is the assembly doing? Do the demeanor and quality of the presider's action and the assembly's action speak of the centrality of the eucharistic prayer? It is to the specific roles of the assembly and presider that we now turn.

NOTES

1. See Consilium for the Implementation of the Constitution on the Liturgy, *Au cours des derniers mois*, in DOL 244, # 1956.

2. Bishops of France, "Great is the Mystery of Faith," in *Origins* 9:30 (10 January 1980): 479.

3. See GIRM 55 and *Aux cours des derniers mois*, DOL 244, #1956.

4. Jean Corbon, *The Wellspring of Worship* (New York: Paulist, 1988), 37.

5. A. Schmemann, *The Eucharist: Sacrament of the Kingdom* (Crestwood, N.Y.: St. Vladimir's Seminary Press, 1988), 169.

6. Enrico Mazza, *The Eucharistic Prayers of the Roman Rite*, trans. M. J. O'Connell (New York: Pueblo, 1986), 42.

7. Jungmann, 111.

8. Mazza, 76.

9. Mazza, 43.

10. Annie Dillard, *Holy the Firm* (New York: Harper and Row, 1977), 45.

11. In what follows on the supper narrative, anamnesis, and the epiclesis, I am drawing on the important work of both Cesare Giraudo and the late Edward J. Kilmartin. See Cesare Giraudo, *Eucaristia per la chiesa: prospettive teologiche sull'eucaristia a partire dalla «lex orandi»* (Rome: Gregorian University Press and Morcelliana, 1989). E. J. Kilmartin, "Catholic Tradition of Eucharistic Theology," *Proceedings of the North American Academy of Liturgy* (1994): 35 – 59; and "The Catholic Tradition of Eucharistic Theology: Towards the Third Millennium," *Theological Studies* 55 (1994): 405 – 457. See also the exposition of Hans Bernhard Meyer, *Eucharistie: Geschichte, Theologie, Pastoral*, vol. 4 of *Gottesdienst der Kirche* (Regensburg: Friedrich Pustet, 1989), 441–460.

12. Corbon, 102.

13. Mazza, 177.

14. This understanding of the supper narrative that emerges from the church's law of prayer is dependent on the work of Giraudo, 329 – 360; here 344.

15. David N. Power, "The Anamnesis: Remembering We Offer," in Senn, 165.

16. See P. Jounel, "La Composition des prières eucharistiques," *La Maison-Dieu* 94 (1968): 75, and James Dallen, "The Congregation's Share in the Eucharistic Prayer," in *Living Bread, Saving Cup*, ed. Kevin Seasoltz (Collegeville: Liturgical Press, 1987), 117.

17. *Music in Catholic Worship*, #53.

18. See Power, "Anamnesis," 149 –150.

19. J. B. Metz, *Faith in History and Society* (New York: Seabury, 1980), 200.

20. F. Senn, "Intercessions and Commemorations in the Anaphora," in Senn, 201.

21. Mazza, 3.

22. Gail Ramshaw, *Words Around the Table* (Chicago: Liturgy Training Publications, 1991), 121.

23. *Au cours des derniers mois*, DOL 244, #1957.

24. Foreword to *Eucharistic Prayers for Masses with Children and for Masses of Reconciliation*.

25. Foreword to *Eucharistic Prayers for Masses with Children and for Masses of Reconciliation*.

26. Christopher Coyne, "Eucharistic Prayers for Masses with Children: Some Observations," *liturgical ministry* 4 (Summer 1995): 115.

27. Mazza's deft rendering of the theme, 216.

28. Mazza, 216.

29. See T. Talley's positive remarks about the prayer in "Structures des anaphores anciennes et modernes," *La Maison-Dieu* 191 (1992): 41–43.

30. On the notion of "ritual field," see Ronald Grimes, *Beginnings in Ritual Studies* (Lanham, Md.: University Press, 1982), 21–32.

31. See M. M. Kelleher, "Liturgy: An Ecclesial Act of Meaning," *Worship* 59 (1985): 482–497.

32. *Music in Catholic Worship*, #6.

33. A. Kavanagh, *Elements of Rite* (New York: Pueblo, 1982), 14.

34. Kavanagh, 21–22.

35. See National Conference of Catholic Bishops, *This Holy and Living Sacrifice: Directory for the Celebration and Reception of Communion under Both Kinds* (Washington, D.C.: USCC, 1985), #39–43.

36. GIRM, #235; *Ceremonial of Bishops*, #86; see the Pastoral Introduction, #58.

37. See the work of E. Foley and M. McGann, *Music and the Eucharistic Prayer* (Collegeville: Liturgical Press, 1988), 20–21.

38. The "principle of progressive solemnity" refers to the notion of more solemn or fuller celebration at more festive times of the liturgical cycle or week. See the *General Instruction of the Liturgy of the Hours*, 273 in DOL 426, #3703.

THE ASSEMBLY'S ROLE

Deeply loved flesh" — that is what we are, "flesh that weeps, laughs; flesh that dances on bare feet in grass."[1] There is no getting around the fact that we are embodied. God fashioned us from the clay of the earth and breathed into us that which animates body and soul. And what God created is very good indeed: flesh and bone, heart and liver, brain and breast, hand and foot. The psalmist knew it well:

> You created every part of me,
> knitting me in my mother's womb.
> For such handiwork, I praise you.
> Awesome this great wonder!
> I see it so clearly! Psalm 139:13–14

As God's fearfully and wonderfully made creatures, we assemble bodily on Sunday to praise and thank God for all that God has done, for God's eternal Word made flesh who leapt down from the heavens. Jesus was indeed flesh: laughing at a wedding feast, weeping at the death of a loved one, spitting on earth and smearing mud on eyes, embracing the outcast, breaking bread at table with friends, being nailed to the cross, suffering death, harrowing hell, being raised to life and breathing out the Spirit.

And we are what Christ is because we are baptized flesh. Our baptism into Christ Jesus forges our new covenant relationship with God. St. Paul reminds us:

> Do you not know that all of us who have been baptized into
> Christ Jesus were baptized into his death? Therefore we have

been buried with him by baptism into death, so that, just as Christ was raised from the dead by the glory of the Father, so we too might walk in newness of life. Romans 6:3–4

Our baptism radically redirects our way of being and living. As baptized flesh, we are "always carrying in the body the death of Jesus, so that the life of Jesus may also be made visible in our bodies" (2 Corinthians 4:10). This is what praying the eucharistic prayer entails. Gathering on Sunday to pray the eucharistic prayer is not one option among many. It is demanded by our baptism. That is what "Sunday obligation" must mean for Catholics.

Praying the eucharistic prayer means that we who carry bodily the death of the Lord empty ourselves before God like Jesus, who "emptied himself . . . obeying to the death, death on the cross" (Philippians 2:7–8). In our doxology, our praise and memorial thanksgiving, we open ourselves to God's way of being and acting in history. We lose ourselves in praise to the author of all. In our obedience to Christ's command to remember, we conform ourselves to his obedience to the Father. Emptied in obedience, we actually become part of Jesus' response to the Father through the grace of the Holy Spirit, who is our voice.

Praying the eucharistic prayer, we baptized manifest our identity as the Body of Christ when we stand before God as a praying assembly. Baptism forges the new covenant relationship with God in Christ through the Spirit: We live now as members of the Body of Christ. Thus baptism creates among us a relationship of communion that is founded on our relationship to Christ through the Spirit.[2] We are adopted by God and fashioned into Christ's body. For we who have been anointed by the Holy Spirit are indeed "other Christs," icons of the Anointed One.[3]

As we proclaim our identity as the Body of Christ, we make visible his life by committing ourselves to be broken and poured out for the life of the world. Our memorial thanksgiving of the death and resurrection of Jesus, into which we have been plunged, must be the pattern of our living. Through our service, by our compassion and in our love for one another, we bring life forth from suffering, we become living sacrifices of praise to God. The "ritual memory of Jesus' death and resurrection is not

Christian unless it is verified in an existential memory whose place is not other that the believer's body."[4] In the words of St. Paul, "For while we live, we are always being given up to death for Jesus' sake, so that the life of Jesus may be made visible in our mortal flesh" (2 Corinthians 4:11). What we sing, shout and proclaim at eucharist — that Christ has trampled death by death — we must sing, shout and proclaim with our very lives.

Eucharistic Presence

The body of Christ offered to Christians in consecrated bread and wine is not something but some*one*. In the eucharist, Christ is present not as an "object" to be admired but as a person (a "subject") to be encountered. Thomas Aquinas understood this well, and so insisted that the ultimate intent (the *res*) of celebrating eucharist is not to produce the sacred species purposes of reservation or adoration, but to create that united body of Christ which is the church. Roman Catholic eucharistic tradition thus insists that the Christological cannot be separated from the ecclesiological. The body of Christ is not only "on" the table but "at" the table!

The body of Christ that is at the table (that is, the church, the *ecclesia*) must be understood as an essential partner in the liturgical act, and not merely as a passive recipient of Christologic benefits. Hence Vatican II's insistence on "full, active, and conscious participation" by the people in eucharistic worship. We become one with Christ's body only by joining ourselves to the Spirit-filled body of believers through grace, faith, and the paschal sacraments of initiation. Indeed, as the New Testament shows, it was precisely the early church's empir-

ical experience of Christ's continued presence and activity in the Spirit that made Easter faith possible and plausible. Easter is about *both* "what happened to Jesus" and "what happened to those who believe in him." Easter meant not only that "Jesus is risen," but that through the Spirit's power the body of Christ has become a people. . . .

Tensions between Christological and ecclesiological aspects of the Eucharist have dominated Western thinking about Real Presence for centuries. Among medieval theologians, Christology triumphed: The "essential moment" of eucharistic consecration was identified, strictly and exclusively, with the liturgical recitation of Jesus' words (the "words of institution"). In support of their view, medieval glossators were fond of citing patristic authorities, especially Ambrose, who in his sermons to the newly baptized seemed similarly to insist on the consecratory power of Christ's words *(the verba Verbi)*. Theological principle *(lex credendi)* gradually overruled liturgical praxis *(lex orandi)*. The prayer of the people was thought to have no real role in relation to the Real Presence. (Keep in mind that though a single

Praying the eucharistic prayer, then, is part of our "labor of the ongoing passage to 'thanksgiving'" by which we are transformed more and more into children of God, begotten in the womb of the font.[5] Through our celebration of the eucharistic prayer, we are working out our baptismal grace, striving to image more clearly Christ Jesus. When our attitude is transformed more perfectly to that of Christ's, dedicating ourselves

voice proclaims it, the eucharistic prayer is not an individual's possession but *the assembly's act*, as articulated by its presiding minister.) Thus, the larger meaning of the whole eucharistic prayer — its acts of praise, remembrance, and intercession; its prayer that the Spirit transform *both* gifts *and* people; its character as ritual deed of a faith-filled assembly — was reduced to insignificance. . . .

Reclaiming the doctrine of Real Presence thus requires that *ecclesiology* be restored to a eucharistic synthesis that for centuries has been almost exclusively Christological. Nowhere is the need for such restoration more evident than in the relation between the ministry of the ordained priest and the eucharistic celebration. It has become fashionable over the past few years to insist loudly that the presiding priest acts *"in persona Christi."* This insistence may be valid, but it misses an equally important aspect of ministry, viz., that the priest acts *"in persona ecclesiae,"* a point long recognized by our best theologians. Thus, for example, Thomas Aquinas could write that the priest "performs a deed of the entire church in consecrating the Eucharist, because it is a sacrament that belongs to the whole church" *(Commentary on the Sentences*, Bk. IV, d. 24; q. 2, art. 2, ad. 2). Aquinas unambiguously recognized that the very nature of eucharist (hence of ministry, hence of Real Presence) is ecclesiological. "It is by reason of the ecclesiological nature of the eucharist that the priest offers for the whole church," concludes Edward Kilmartin, "not immediately because he offers in the person of Christ." In a word, the priest can "offer Mass" in the first instance because he is a member of the believing assembly. . . .

Real Presence is an essential aspect of eucharistic theology in the Catholic tradition — but "resacralizing reaction" will not reclaim it. We can experience Real Presence anew only by renewing the covenant between Word and World. Catholic sacramentalism can be recovered only if we recognize afresh that human history is a history of meaning; that those meanings are celebrated through rituals of civility; that language is not only revelation, but responsibility and grace as well; that God is celebrating the liturgy of the world — *in us* — through the length and breadth of creation.

to thankfulness (see Colossians 4:2), our whole view of life and the world radically changes. We recognize that in Christ Jesus we have been given every good gift, filled with life and goodness, blessed and made holy (EP I). All we have is sheer gift, even our thanksgiving itself:

> You have no need of our praise, yet our desire to thank you is itself your gift. Our hymn of thanksgiving adds nothing to your greatness, but makes us grow in your grace through Jesus Christ our Lord. Preface for Weekdays IV

The very Spirit of God, whose seal is graven on us, enables us to call God "Abba" (Galatians 4:6). The presence of the Spirit bestowed on the church awakens our memory and inspires our thanksgiving.[6] Indeed we must always remember that the initiative for all of our thanks and praise lies with God.

HOUSEHOLDS OF THANKSGIVING

Praying the eucharistic prayer is difficult work. We cannot expect to show up at Sunday eucharist ready to participate fully, actively and consciously if our lives day in and day out are not lives of thanksgiving. Our active role in the eucharistic prayer begins before we even reach the table. It begins in our homes.

Do we reverence our food and take time for meals? We live in a culture of the instantaneous: faxing and e-mailing, drive-throughs and express lanes, microwaves and automatic teller machines and on-line updates. Can our meals be "that pause in a day's course when creation's bounty and beauty are given a chance to reveal themselves afresh"? Can our meals "not merely refresh our bodies but . . . renew our hearts"?[7]

Once we sit down to table, whether we are with other family members, a loved one or all alone, do we say grace? Do we bless God for so graciously bringing us to that moment, for giving us the breath to speak the prayer and the place to say it? Do we remember how God has been so good to us in the past and ask God to continue to sustain us? Do we name before God at that moment what weighs on our hearts, grieves our minds, shakes our hope? Perhaps we read a short scripture verse before we thank

God and so make clear that the word of God grounds all we do and pray. We are often very good at prayers of petition and supplication. We need to be equally at home with simply blessing God and praising God whose name is excellent in all the earth.

What memories do we keep? Are we attuned to the days and seasons of the natural, civil and liturgical year? Is the book of household blessings well worn?[8] Do we mark anniversaries of baptism? of the death of loved ones? of saints and other holy ones?

Do we give ourselves over to the mystery of God in our daily lives?[9] Are we able to name the presence of God in the ordinary as well as the extraordinary? When things are going well—food is on the table, the car is running, the boss is forgiving, grandmother is home from the hospital and the sun is shining—we might find it easy to breathe a thank you. But are we able to struggle with the more difficult call to see God at work in the difficult times—in our experience of limitation, in illness, in violence, in death? in moments of feeling utterly alone, of hurt? These moments speak even more powerfully of our need for communion with God. Can we boldly name an absent God and call God back to the center of things?

Do we read scripture? Taking the scripture readings for the coming Sunday and reflecting on them during the week can become a spiritual discipline that prepares us for our eucharistic assembly. Do we take up the acclamations of the eucharistic prayer and use them as in our domestic prayer? Can any of the refrains serve as a mantra for centering prayer? Might sections of the eucharistic prayers themselves serve or inspire the way we shape our prayers?

A House under Siege

Living lives of thanksgiving, being a eucharistic people day in and day out, is not an easy calling. In fact, striving to live a life of thanksgiving witnesses prophetically to a world that has a tough time saying thank-you to anyone for anything.

Far from remembering who we are, whose we are, why we are and how far we have come, we forget. And we have forgotten even more:

the power of images and media, respect, intelligence, the family, equality of peoples, the beauty and power of sexuality.[10]

Not only have we forgotten, but more and more we impoverish good human actions: the meal, reading, the conversation of spouses and friends. The great rhythm of life is trivialized as babies and teens are the objects of great marketing projects, the elderly are hushed up in homes and the dead are cosmeticized at our funeral homes.

All of these habits of life in our times are great obstacles to our praying the eucharistic prayer. There have always been such obstacles, such habits of life that are matters for the ongoing work of conversion. Even as we attempt to pray as a eucharistic people, to remember and give

How Do We Give Praise and Thanks?

The voice and manner of the priest should show that he offers this prayer as spokesman for everyone present. It is a *prayer* addressed to the Father. Not a homily or a drama or a talk given to the assembly, it embraces remembrance of God's saving deeds, invocation of the Holy Spirit, the narrative of the Last Supper, remembrance of the church universal and of the dead, and climaxes "through him, with him, in him . . ."

For all our devotion to the body and blood of Christ present on our altars, we Catholics have hardly begun to make this eucharistic prayer the heart of the liturgy. It is still, to all appearances, a monologue by the priest, who stops several times to let the people sing. We seem as yet to have little sense for the flow, the movement, the beauty of the eucharistic prayer. How are we to make our own this prayer which is the summit and center of the church's whole life? How are we to see that this prayer is the model of Christian life and daily prayer? Does this prayer of thanks and praise gather up the way we pray by ourselves every day? When we assemble on Sunday, we help one another learn over and over again how to praise and thank God through and with and in Christ, in good and bad times, until he comes in glory.

Are we a thanks-giving people? Do we give God praise by morning and thanks by night? Do we pause over every table before eating, as we do over this altar table, to bless God and ourselves and our food? The habit of thanksgiving, of praise, of eucharist, must be acquired day by day, not just at Sunday Mass. In fact, it is at Mass that our habits of daily life come to full expression in Christ.

Excerpts from Cardinal Joseph Bernardin, Our Communion, Our Peace, Our Promise: Pastoral Letter on the Liturgy *(also available as* Guide for the Assembly*) (Chicago: Liturgy Training Publications, 1984), pp. 16–17. © 1984 Archdiocese of Chicago: Liturgy Training Publications.*

thanks for the liberation accorded us by Christ's giving himself up to death, we begin to unveil the sin that pervades this world.

THE PRAYER OF THE WHOLE ASSEMBLY

Only as we practice the demanding work of living lives of thanksgiving and striving for ongoing conversion can we can expect to come to the table to pray the eucharistic prayer. Yet only as those who pray that eucharistic prayer can we live such lives.

We begin to glimpse what eucharistic praying in an ordinary parish might be, to realize what full, conscious, active celebration of the eucharistic prayer entails. Do we want to grasp with heart and mind and body that the pasch of Christ is our own mystery? Do we want to know it as within and among us?[11]

Our ritual activity is not an end in itself; rather, it is the means of our bodily engagement with the mystery that is ours because we are Christ's. All our ritual activity is grounded in our continual expression of our baptismal faith.

When we come together to celebrate liturgy, the indispensable means by which we come to know the mystery as graven on our flesh are singing, swaying, processing, acclaiming, smelling, seeing, tasting, touching.[12] Our bodily engagement is not added on to our celebration of the liturgy; it is not a choice or just some nicety. It is crucial to our transformation by the Spirit of the incarnate one, Jesus. Through our hands and feet, arms and legs, all our senses, we come to recognize the advent of the mystery of God in word and action. We first come to it by attending to and discovering it through our bodies. The very tools of liturgy accomplish this: "Festival excess and colors and tastes and textures and odors and forms and touches" raise the covenant community to the realm of new possibility.[13]

The eucharistic prayer is intimately linked to the whole Sunday liturgy, from gathering to opening prayer, from readings to greeting of peace, and from Lord's prayer to final blessing. There is no celebrating community at the eucharistic prayer unless there is such a community throughout. Do we process and sing? Do we pray and listen? When invitations to pray are given, do we take the time to pray?

The general intercessions are a crucial moment at liturgy. From the early days of the Christian churches, the first act of the newly baptized was to raise their hands and join in the prayer of the faithful. Stirred by the word of God that beckons us to recognize the presence of God in our struggle to live here and now, we stand together and pray before we approach the table of thanksgiving. We stand full in our experiences in the world and name in prayer that which pleads with God to act here and now, because we have heard in the word the promise that God acts. We embrace the pain and name the emptiness in our church and world in the prayer of the faithful.

Truly, only after a prayer through which the assembly recognizes itself at the intersection of God's word, the future that word promises and our struggle to so live, can we take the fruits of this world — bread and wine — and sing our great thanks to God in the awesome memory of the pasch. We too often miss that the prayer of the faithful is what we the assembly do in the depths of our hearts when we are bidden by the deacon or cantor. We then give it voice in our response, and the prayer flows forth from our frame.

A particular danger with regard to the assembly's role in the eucharistic prayer arises from using theater or drama as an analogy to liturgy. While many are well intentioned, these theater or drama analogies have worked against authentic celebration, especially at the eucharistic prayer. As we have seen, the eucharistic prayer is not a dramatic reenactment of the Last Supper, nor is it any sort of play-acting. There is no room for a spectator mentality, as if we the assembly could sit back like an audience at a musical.

Nor is this participation of ours to join in something someone else does. We baptized gather together as church, the Body of Christ locally gathered. This concrete assembly of the baptized is the subject and agent of every liturgical celebration.[14] As the GIRM emphasizes, "Every liturgical celebration . . . is an action of Christ the priest and of his Body, which is the church" (26). This is the full measure of what is meant by participation: The whole body joined together celebrates.[15] Authentic participation means that the assembly articulates its baptismal identity.

Yet, authentic participation should not be translated into "ritual busyness." Increased numbers of acclamations, gestures and songs can be self-conscious activity instead of ritual engagement with the mystery of grace.[16] So, too, swayed by prevailing cultural forces, some have concluded that if the assembly is not doing something or the same thing at the same time, it is not participating. "Giving the people something to do" somehow assures that they are celebrating. Active participation allows for silence, listening, praying, assuming a posture. Our ritual behavior must both go beyond the surface to deeper conversion to the mystery of Christ and give bodily expression to the mystery at work within us.

AN ORDERED ASSEMBLY

A central impediment to the assembly's claiming its role is this: The ordered character of the church gathered is mistaken or forgotten. Our assemblies are, in the words of the council, "hierarchically ordered assemblies."[17] As Paul imagines us, we are one body with many members, each with different ministries to build up the unity of the body. The *Constitution on the Sacred Liturgy* emphasizes:

> Liturgical services are not private functions, but are celebrations belonging to the church, which is the "sacrament of unity," namely, the holy people united and ordered under their bishops. (26)

There is no doubt that when the liturgical assembly gathers, the whole church celebrates: "The whole people celebrate the word, but this does not mean that everyone must proclaim together the readings or give the homily. The whole people celebrate the eucharist . . . but this does not mean that everyone must recite the eucharistic prayer. Likewise, the whole people sing, but each according to his or her charism."[18] A mistaken or one-sided approach to the character of our Christian assembly neglects the importance of roles in the liturgical assembly.

Thus, though the whole assembly celebrates and prays the eucharistic prayer, one member of the body gives it voice because that person is the presider of the assembly, called and ordered by the bishop. The praying of the eucharistic prayer is the work of all the baptized; the voicing of the prayer in the assembly is the work of the ordained minister. What has been crucial to the church here is that the character and central importance of this singular prayer be manifest. The requirement that the prayer be voiced by one ordained and representing the bishop testifies to our need to manifest always that this is the church at prayer. The ordained presider who proclaims the prayer brings to expression "the holy communion of the church in Christ's body and blood."[19]

> A communally recited eucharistic prayer is a gross abuse because it fails to express the fact that the church prays together as one people "hierarchically assembled." When the prayer is communally recited, its very use fails to express a Catholic understanding of the nature of the church.[20]

As we have gleaned from the eucharistic prayers themselves, the ritual act of praying the eucharistic prayer is a manifestation of the church, the Body of Christ, head and members. The role of the presider is crucial because "the presiding action of bishop or priest incarnates, makes tangible, the communion, the joined hands, of all the churches."[21]

The presider and the assembly gather together as church. They cannot manifest the reality of the church without one another. So, while grasping the place of the presider, the assembly must engage itself in the praying of the prayer.

Toward Embodying the Eucharistic Prayer

The assembly's first means of engaging in the praying of the eucharistic prayer is through posture. "The groundwork of prayer is laid in our bodies."[22] As baptized flesh, our vocation is to give flesh, bone and breath of life to our eucharistic prayer. Our bodily posture is the visible expression of our interior lives of thanksgiving and praise. As GIRM, 21 states:

At every Mass the people should stand . . . from the prayer over the gifts to the end of Mass, except . . . [t]hey should kneel *(genuflectant)* at the consecration unless prevented by the lack of space, the number of people present, or some other good reason.

When queried about people kneeling from the Holy, Holy until the end of the prayer, Roman authorities quite firmly stated that:

[The] purpose is to ensure uniformity in posture in the assembly celebrating the eucharist as a manifestation of the community's unity in faith and worship. The people often give the impression immediately after the Sanctus and even more after the consecration by their diverse postures that they are unmindful of being participants in the church's liturgy, which is the supreme action of the community and not a time for individuals to isolate themselves in acts of private devotion.[23]

Thus, "the ancient practice of standing for the prayer has thus been restored as the norm, but the thirteenth-century exception (kneeling at the [Institution narrative]) has nevertheless been maintained."[24] However, the bishops of the United States adapted this rubric, deciding that "[number] 21 of the GIRM should be adapted so that the people kneel beginning at after the singing or recitation of the Sanctus until after the Amen of the eucharistic prayer, that is, before the Lord's prayer."[25] The reason for the departure from the posture called for by the GIRM was concern at the time of the reform that too much change at once would not be absorbed by the people.[26] The reasons had nothing to do with fear of irreverence, nor were they theological reasons. The issue was burdening the people with too many reforms at once.

However, those days have long passed. Posture gives bodily expression to our understanding of the eucharist. Kneeling, a posture of humility, supplication and adoration, bespeaks an understanding of eucharistic praying that emphasizes the activity of the priest and adoration of the Lord present in the eucharistic elements. However, if the conciliar mandate of active participation in worship grounded in baptism is taken seriously, if we have a theology of the eucharistic prayer as the active self-engagement of the whole assembly in the pasch of Christ ordered to communion, then standing is the most appropriate posture.

We are called to exercise the fullness of our vocation; we stand baptized. We come bidden by the Lord's command to remember; we stand obedient. We gather on Sunday to feast at the Lord's pasch from death to life; we stand risen from the stinking tomb of sin and death. We gather to give thanks and praise; we stand ready and willing. We behold the Holy

Standing: A Posture of Reverence

Many meanings: Standing is a posture used in our society to express respect between persons. One usually stands, and a group of people often stand, when a respected person enters the room, for example, while a dignitary makes an official entrance. The citizens of a nation stand during the national anthem, denoting a common identity and a sense of "owning" a nationality, a sense of being a part of the nation. Standing can define a relationship, such as standing in the presence of someone in authority; standing can also symbolize one's readiness to act at the request of such a person. Standing can mean being prepared to serve when called on, as does someone waiting on tables in a restaurant. Standing is also a position of a prisoner being sentenced, the soldier receiving orders, or of one bringing gifts, (M. Searle, "On Gestures," *Liturgy* [London] 7 [December 1982-January 1983], 55). There are idiomatic expressions that reflect what standing means: to stand up for what we believe or for what is right, that we won't stand for nonsense, or we expect something to be laid at our feet ("Gestures and Symbols," *National Bulletin on Liturgy*, vol. 17, no. 94 [May-June 1984], 152).

STANDING IS THE ORIGINAL GESTURE OF PRAYER, the *Urgebärde,* used by people of all cultures, according to Gruen and Reepen. It is a position in which we can direct ourselves to God rather than turning inward, opening up to his presence, and allowing ourselves to be filled with his Spirit. This posture also leaves one more free to use the hands in gestures of prayer.

PROCLAMATION OF THE GOSPEL: Some insight into the posture of standing as a gesture of reverence can be gained by reflection on the custom of standing for the proclamation of the gospel, a requirement that has been maintained throughout the whole of the history of the Roman rite. The church sees the gospel as Christ himself speaking to his people (GIRM, 9).

REVERENCE: Standing at the eucharistic prayer then can be a posture of reverence in the same sense. Since word and sacrament are one act of worship, and it is the same Christ who in the gospel speaks to the church and then in the eucharist offers himself with the church to the Father, the same gesture of reverence would be in order.

One of God in our midst; we stand reverent and attentive. We are called to be broken and poured out in service; we stand ready. We await Christ coming again in glory; we stand vigilant. In light of history and theology, and in light of the very nature of eucharistic praying itself, standing "is the posture that most befits active participation. . . . Standing is no abuse of the law; in fact it serves better the value of active participation than does kneeling."[27]

A SINGLE PRAYER: Standing throughout the whole of the prayer also respects the form of the prayer, which begins with the dialogue in which the people are invited to lift up their hearts and at the end affirm the prayer with their "Amen." The prayer is seen as a unit, as one prayer of praise and thanksgiving, and the whole of it is being seen as consecratory (J. Dallen, "The Congregation's Share in the Eucharistic Prayer," *Worship* 52 [July 1978]: 329).

PRAYER OF THE WHOLE CHURCH: The eucharistic prayer is also the prayer of the whole church, the prayer of the Body of Christ; because it belongs to the whole community it is a presidential prayer, the presider praying not in place of the community but with the community. Standing has now again become the accepted posture for the other presidential prayers; for the eucharistic prayer, the most important of the presidential prayers, the community would want to be united in posture with the one praying with them, symbolizing through the posture of standing that it "owns" the prayer proclaimed by the presider. (It has not been seen as irreverent on the part of the presider to be standing for this prayer.)

FOSTERING PARTICIPATION: Participation on the part of the people in the present eucharistic prayers needs to be fostered through the ways available, listening and singing the acclamations. Both of these modes of participation can be done better in a standing position. In fact, standing while singing is taken for granted; note the regulation in 1502 that recommended standing rather than kneeling when there was singing at Mass.

SHAPED BY THE LITURGY: There is one more angle to consider. We do not merely shape the liturgy; the liturgy shapes us. It shapes our attitudes toward God and to one another (Searle, 58). We must ask then what do our postures say to us, whether what our body is doing says what is expressed, or whether it contradicts it. Our posture does not just show reverence to Christ in the eucharistic elements; our posture shows reverence to what the liturgy is about, the celebration of praise and thanks to God through Christ by the whole assembly. Our posture shows reverence ultimately to the paschal mystery; it celebrates the resurrection, Christ's presence among us, and the parousia that was so uppermost in the minds of the early Christians.

Excerpts from Zita Maier, "Standing at Eucharist: A Posture of Reverence," National Bulletin on Liturgy vol. 28, no. 140 (1995). *Copyright © Concacan Inc. All rights reserved. Used by permission of the Canadian Conference of Catholic Bishops, Ottawa, Canada.*

Changing posture alone, however, is not suddenly going to make the eucharistic prayer the prayer of the whole church gathered, presider and assembly. What must first be transformed is the assembly's and the presider's grasp of their baptismal dignity, the meaning of the eucharistic prayer and a conversion to a eucharistic way of living and praying. Then the posture will truly embody the prayer.

The current discipline of a "split" posture, with the presider and deacon standing and the assembly standing, then kneeling, must be acknowledged as less than the best solution. If standing during the eucharistic prayer is acknowledged as a legitimate adaptation and not an abuse of the law, then all should stand from the prayer over the gifts through the Amen. If kneeling is the only option for the assembly, then they should kneel from the dialogue through the Amen. The eucharistic prayer is a single prayer; changes in posture undermine this unity.

In GIRM, 21 the word translated "kneel" (genuflectant) is the same word translated as "genuflect" when the presider is the subject. It would seem legitimate that if an assembly that stands throughout the prayer discerns that a gesture at the supper narrative is appropriate, all might genuflect when the presider genuflects. Impeded by the number of people present, all might bow profoundly.

Moreover, we do not stand any which way, as if were waiting in line at the grocery store — fidgety, slouched and slovenly. Likewise, we do not kneel slumped over or using the pew as a stool. Changing posture alone will not make all the difference, but changing posture with good catechesis will. Attitudes will be changed by reflection and by experience. To stand aright for eucharistic prayer means that one stands alert, vigilant, attentive, ready to move to the promised land. We stand ready, obedient and attentive to the God who calls us to the wedding feast of the Lamb. We stand beckoning the Spirit to tether us in communion.

A little choreography could make all the difference. All could assume the ancient prayer position, known as the "praying," or *orans*, position: hands uplifted to the height of one's head with the palms facing outward and slightly upward.[28] Our uplifted hands — whether we are on our knees or standing upright — embody our doxology: We lift up our hearts, we lift up our praise, we lift up our thanksgiving as we lift up our hands. We bask in the beautiful light of the Son of God made flesh. We are struck with awe by the mighty deeds our God has done and still does. We plead that the Spirit of love come. The *Catechism of the Catholic Church* describes such a posture:

> In the catacombs, the church is often represented as a woman in prayer, arms outstretched in the praying position. Like Christ who stretched out his arms on the cross, through him, with him, and in him, she offers herself and intercedes for all. (1368)

What more appropriate stance could we take to pray the eucharistic prayer! We who recall Christ's pasch show forth the empty cross with our very bodies, bodies marked with that cross at our baptism.

Standing: Vigilance and Action

In the first place, to stand up means that we are in possession of ourselves. Instead of sitting relaxed and at ease, we take hold of ourselves; we stand, as it were, at attention, geared and ready for action.

Standing is the other side of reverence toward God. Kneeling is the side of worship in rest and quietness; standing is the side of vigilance and action. It is the respect of the servant in attendance, of the soldier on duty.

When the good news of the gospel is proclaimed, we stand up. Godparents stand when in the child's place they make the solemn profession of faith, children when they renew these promises at their first communion. Bridegroom and bride stand when they bind themselves at the altar to be faithful to their marriage vow. On these and like occasions we stand up.

Even when we are praying alone, to pray standing may more forcibly express our inward state. The early Christians stood by preference. The "Orante," in the familiar catacomb representation, stands in her long flowing robes of a woman of rank and prays with outstretched hands, in perfect freedom, perfect obedience, quietly attending to the word, and in readiness to perform it with joy.

We may feel at times a sort of constraint in kneeling. One feels freer standing up, and in that case standing is the right position. But stand up straight: not leaning, both feet on the ground, the knees firm, not slackly bent, upright, in control. Prayer made thus is both free and obedient, both reverent and serviceable.

Excerpts from Romano Guardini, Sacred Signs *(Michael Glazier, 1956), pp. 21–23. © 1956 Michael Glazier.*

Any change of posture — whether from kneeling to kneeling with *orans* or from kneeling to standing — requires careful, sensitive pastoral formation. Pastoral teams need to acknowledge that if the bodily in worship is downplayed, then any change in posture will be perceived as precious or even heterodox. If we do not plunge adults and infants into the waters of baptism, if we do not anoint with abandon our sick, if we do not lay hands on the sinner, if we do not process, if we never reverence the gathered assembly with incense or sprinkle with water, if we do not use bread and wine, then our assemblies will never realize that "it is all right — believe it or not — to be people."[29] Only then will standing upright with arms in prayer come near to embodying an assembly's prayer. Some members of the assembly may be physically prevented from standing by age or health; they should understand that we pray as we are able and give bodily expression to our prayer as we can. If some members must sit for a legitimate reason, they should understand that though the flesh is weak, the Spirit is able and willing. All are called to "shun any appearance of individualism or division" (GIRM, 62). To those who clamor that such posture is uncomfortable, whether for physical or pious reasons, recall that "Jesus Christ's incarnate presence caused notable discomfort even for those who loved him best."[30]

SINGING, SHOUTING, SAYING

The most excellent way that the assembly embodies its eucharistic praying is through the full-throated singing of the acclamations of the prayer: the Holy, Holy, the memorial acclamation and the Amen. It still bears repeating that these acclamations, even if the whole prayer itself is not sung, demand sung performance by their very nature. The unity of the eucharistic prayer as a movement from dialogue to doxology demands that the musical settings of the acclamations ordinarily used be of the same melody, or "setting." The common melody from Holy, Holy to Amen establishes a movement that exemplifies the unity of the prayer.

The acclamations demand sung performance because music embodies thanksgiving in a way similar to posture. Singing the common

acclamations unites the assembly by a common breathing that shows forth the unity of its action: joining with the choirs of heaven, proclaiming the mystery of faith and assenting to the whole prayer. Music engages our bodies in a way that simple speech cannot. To sing shifts our posture and shakes our created frame. Singing engages muscle and breath and heart and soul. It wells up from our core, moves us to joy and tears. We, the Spirit-filled Body of Christ, as best we can, sing forth by the power of the Spirit, who can turn even the flattest groans into glorias.

Not just any music will do. With so many choices available, the competent musician must realize that the music of the acclamations must, like the acclamations themselves, be forceful and meaningful. Three helpful criteria for evaluating music for the eucharistic prayer are:[31]

- Does the music serve the proclamation of the prayer? The goal is to find music that is wedded to text, a unity that is experienced as such essentially, by singing.

■ Does the music engage the assembly in such a way that the prayer is experienced as an action of the gathered assembly?

■ Does the music contribute to a sense of the prayer as a unified whole?

If we take seriously that the eucharistic prayer is the center and summit of the liturgy, then any preparation for music at liturgy must begin with the acclamations for the eucharistic prayer. From that starting point, one can then relate the prayer to the rest of the celebration with transition from the preparation of the gifts to the prayer, or from the prayer to the communion rite, and then outward to the gathering and dismissal.[32] Is the praise of the Holy, Holy echoed in the Gloria or in the Alleluia? Is the resounding acclamation of the pasch reinforced in the communion song? Is the fervor of the Amen taken up in the gathering?

To grasp what is at stake with regard to the acclamations, we need first to recall their crucial function. "The acclamations . . . create a degree of the active participation that the gathered faithful must contribute in every form of the Mass, in order to express clearly and to further the entire community's involvement" (GIRM, 15). The acclamations to the eucharistic prayers of the Roman rite are part of the prayer itself. They are not add-ons or "responses" to what the presider says. They constitute an integral part of the prayer.[33] The assembly joins in the celestial prayer praise, voices its remembrance and hope, gives its assent.

The acclamations give the assembly a sense of ownership of the prayer, and musicians must be careful not to usurp that ownership in the name of variety. In a parish with basic musical resources, one good set of eucharistic acclamations that everyone knows by heart may be all that is needed. The varying seasons can be marked by the use of instrumentation or harmonization. In a parish where the assembly has more musical experience and leadership, perhaps two or three sets of acclamations might be in order, to vary with the liturgical seasons.

Even in parishes with many Sunday Masses and a variety of musical genres at those Masses—or even a variety of cultural expressions—a common set of eucharistic acclamations that anyone who goes to any

Mass could sing from the heart is the goal. The acclamations should be so well known that any printed music program would be superfluous. The acclamations should be so well known that the assembly could take up parts or all of them in daily prayer.

Many new settings of acclamations have been introduced that are arranged so that the cantor sings a refrain and the assembly repeats it. Great caution should be exercised when approaching such compositions. The role of the cantor may be important in the initial stages of learning the acclamations, but the cantor who sings a line of the acclamation that the assembly then repeats needlessly removes the assembly one step from its ministry and threatens to obscure the assembly's role in acclaiming, which is primary. The assembly should know its acclamations, its expression of its role, so well that the intervention of a cantor is quite unnecessary. As for settings that ascribe sections to the choir or to soloists, it might

The Assembly's Song

The people's singing possesses a particular beauty that even the most perfectly trained choir cannot attain. Of course, the people sometimes drag out the final note, fail to observe the eighth-notes, upset the melody, bellow the high notes—all defects that call be corrected in time. But we must not judge the people's singing solely by the criteria that may be used for the choir. The assembly is not a choir placed in the nave; the assembly is the people of God. When the choir sings, all the people listen, and if the choir's execution is mediocre, the people notice. The assembly's prayer is disturbed, and the people have the right to criticize. But when the whole assembly sings, no one listens—except God—for everyone joins in as an expression of his or her participation in the liturgy. It is in this union of all the voices present that the particular beauty of the assembly's singing resides: the innocent voices of the children, croaking voices of the elderly, voices that are well placed, voices that are nasal. All these numerous, diverse voices express what no single voice can express alone: the mystery of the church that unites everyone in common praise of Christ, so that as Paul wrote to the Christians of Rome, "together you may with one voice glorify the God and Father of our Lord Jesus Christ" (Romans 15:6).

Excerpts from Lucien Deiss, Visions of Liturgy and Music for a New Century (Collegeville: Liturgical Press, 1996), pp. 39–40. © 1996 Liturgical Press. Used with permission.

be best not be to use these: "From the viewpoint of the assembly . . . their exclusion from the song which is only performed by other ministers communicates at the level of public meaning that the assembly is not only less important . . . but that the assembly itself is not integral or necessary."[34] There is certainly a place for the alternating of assembly and choir or assembly and cantor, but not here. As the assembly struggles to recover what eucharistic praying is about and embody the prayer through sung acclamation, such compositions are better suited for other moments in the liturgy. At the eucharistic prayer, the music must communicate that the assembly and the music ministers are bound together.[35]

Some are nostalgic for the chant Masses of the *Liber Usualis* sung by the choir, or they are moved by the choir's virtuosity with a polyphonic or Baroque setting of the Sanctus. Such a contribution by the choir is deeply valued but is best reserved for other times. We are concerned with acclamations, and "beauty alone does not transform melody into an acclamation."[36] The crucial function of the people's active participation in the acclamation must be more valued than the beauty of polyphony or chant. The choir must not take the place of the assembly.[37] The body of everyone in the assembly should resound and shout forth praise, the breath of life entering dry bones.

ADDING ADDITIONAL ACCLAMATIONS

Taking the lead from the eucharistic prayers for Masses with Children and the initiative of musicians, some assemblies are adding additional acclamations to the eucharistic prayer at Sunday Mass. As the introduction to the prayers for Masses with Children notes, "the number of acclamations in the eucharistic prayers for Masses with Children has been increased, in order to enlarge this kind of participation and make it more effective."[38] *The Mass of Creation* is perhaps the best-known example of the way these acclamations are introduced: additional "hosanna" or other seasonal refrains like "alleluia" or "glory to God in the highest," repetition of the memorial acclamation, some type of intercessory refrain like "Lord, have mercy" or "hear our prayer."[39]

However, under the current discipline in the United States, assemblies, musicians or presiders are not at liberty to add additional acclamations to the eucharistic prayers that do not provide for them. At the time of this writing, the only eucharistic prayers that allow for additional acclamations are the eucharistic prayers for Masses with Children, which, we have seen are not for use with adult assemblies, and the eucharistic prayer for Masses for Various Needs and Occasions in its musical setting. The permission that had been granted for settings of the eucharistic prayer like the *Mass of Creation* setting of EP III is not rescinded, but any addition of acclamations to the existing prayers must be done by the Bishops' Committee on the Liturgy.[40] There are two sides to this coin.

On the one hand, many assemblies have found that the addition of acclamations gives them a greater sense of participation and ownership of the eucharistic prayer. Many report that the acclamations, especially when varied according to the shifts in the prayer, have made them aware of the styles of language in the prayer and its movement from thanksgiving to supplication. Also, the frequent musical intervention makes the prayer a more solemn and festive event, especially if there has been strong or lengthy music in the rest of the liturgy.

Yet there is also wisdom in cautious reserve. Those who find pastoral value in the addition of acclamations need to take the following points seriously: First, acclamations generally mark movements in the prayer. They are punctuations from praise to thanksgiving to supplication.[41] This means that there is no acclamation for the sake of acclamation. The acclamations are integral parts of the prayer, the assembly's share in the movement. To move, add or rearrange acclamations does not just give the assembly a more active role; it could change the dynamics of its prayer. Second, acclamations are acclamations, not responses. That is to say, the assembly is not merely responding to something the presider says, but they are actually taking part in the whole of the prayer itself.

A way that some assemblies have found to balance the need for more vocal involvement and for respecting the dynamic of the eucharistic prayer is to turn to its original cry of assent: the Amen. Amen is the assembly's "so be it" to the presider's voicing of its prayer. These Amen acclamations can be carefully scored at points of transition and logical breaks in the prayer. They are effective, though, only if the whole prayer is sung (see page 114). The presider may initially elicit the assembly's Amen, but gradually the assembly comes to know the shifts in the prayer and the rise and fall of the chant and spontaneously sings Amen at the proper times. An advantage to using a repeated Amen is this: It focuses attention on the text being assented to, rather than the interjection itself. Great care should be taken to ensure that the final Amen is indeed the "Great

Amen as Acclamation

Amen means "What you have said is true" and "So be what you have said." Amen, the original acclamation of the eucharistic prayer, is the assembly's assent to what the presider voices as the prayer of the church. Some assemblies have found that extending the use of Amen through the sung eucharistic prayer—not just at the end—fosters more attentive, conscious participation in eucharistic praying. What follows is an example (using Eucharistic Prayer III in the 1985 sacramentary) of where the sung Amen might be expanded. It is important that these Amen acclamations come at the proper ritual moments in the prayer. Initially the presider might cue the assembly by singing the Amen, which the assembly affirms. Very soon though, the cues become unnecessary as the assembly comes to know the flow of the prayer.

Presider	All
It is truly right and just that in all things we should give you thanks, eternal God, and in every season proclaim your mighty deeds. . . .	Holy, Holy, Holy, . . .
Father, you are holy indeed, . . . by the working of the Holy Spirit.	Amen!
From age to age . . . to the glory of your name.	Amen!
And so, Father, we bring you these gifts,	Amen!

Amen" by repeating it several times and reinforcing it with strong musical accompaniment or harmonization.

More importantly, we must be certain that acclamations do not become the only means of active participation: Are we making them bear more than they can while we neglect the meaning of participation as embodying the mystery of Christ's pasch? So, too, they may be working against the eucharistic prayer itself: "The impression is given that the acclamations constitute the peak experiences of the prayer viewed from the standpoint of interest and community participation, whereas the basic content of the prayer itself is secondary and unengaging."[42]

Presider	All
We ask . . . at whose command we celebrate this eucharist.	Amen!
On the night . . . this is my body which will be given up for you.	Amen!
When supper was ended, . . . so that sins may be forgiven.	Amen!
Do this in memory of me.	Amen!
Let us proclaim the mystery of faith.	Christ has died, . . .
Father, calling to mind . . . we offer you in thanksgiving this holy and living sacrifice.	Amen!
Look with favor . . . to reconcile us to yourself.	Amen!
Grant that we . . . one spirit in Christ.	Amen!
May he make us . . . intercession we rely for help.	Amen!
Lord, may this sacrifice . . . your Son has gained for you.	Amen!
Father, hear . . . they may be.	Amen!
Welcome into . . . your friendship.	Amen!
We hope to enjoy . . . good things come.	
Through him . . . for ever and ever.	Amen, Amen, Amen!

Instrumental Music and the Eucharistic Prayer

In an attempt to boost the musical character of the eucharistic prayer, some musicians play music underneath the spoken sections of the prayer. Thus, after the dialogue to the prayer is spoken, piano or other music is played under the spoken preface before the Holy, Holy is sung, and so on. If there are acclamations that are interspersed throughout the prayer, then the instrumental music can sustain unity, creating a fabric of music and text, spoken and sung. Parishes need a very skilled musician who can do the improvisation well and employ chordal underlay.

If there are no additional acclamations, this instrumental music probably should not be done. While the provision of GIRM, 12 that "while the priest is reciting [presidential] prayers there should be no other prayer, and the organ or other instruments should not be played" is directed to curb preconciliar practices when the language of the liturgy was unintelligible to the assembly and many prayers were prayed inaudibly, it has application today.[43] Unless the music is supporting the singing of the prayer, the acclamations, or their transition, musicians would best keep custody of their hands. The paradigm is not an elevator or cocktail lounge background sound. That is not what music and eucharistic praying are about.

Music ministers do need to pay careful attention to this problem: how to move immediately from the presider's spoken or sung text to the acclamation. Delays for instrumental introductions break the flow and should be completely unacceptable. The acclamation must come at once, almost falling over the last words of the presider. Either the musical introductions could be played very gently and quietly under the last words of the cue, or there is no introduction, just the beginning of the acclamation from a cantor. If the acclamations are good music and are used regularly, that will suffice to bring in the whole assembly.

Living Sacrifice of Praise

We are baptized flesh; we stand before God in thanksgiving and we manifest our identity as the Body of Christ. That is who we are and what we do.

We come to our eucharistic praying from our day-to-day living—full of thanksgiving while bearing bodily the death of the Lord. When we gather as baptized flesh to pray the eucharistic prayer, the goal of our full, conscious, active participation is this: that the "pray-er becomes the prayer"![44]

We embody eucharistic praying in our attitude, our posture and our song. Even at those times when we listen to the presider who gathers our voices into one, our listening requires far more of us than we think. We who are baptized "attend . . . with the ear of [our]heart."[45] We listen with the ear of our heart that we might be transformed by the mystery we name and celebrate. The eucharistic prayer is indeed the prayer of the whole church gathered, by which we become more by the power of the Spirit whom we ask God to send. Yet as utterly crucial as our role is, we are the whole church gathered and we need careful, prayerful leadership. That will be the concern of the next chapter.

NOTES

1. Toni Morrison, *Beloved* (New York: Knopf, 1988), 88–89.

2. See L.-M. Chauvet, *Symbol and Sacrament: A Sacramental Reinterpretation of Christian Existence,* trans. P. Madigan and M. Beaumont (Collegeville: Liturgical Press, 1995), 439–440.

3. See the third mystagogical catechesis ascribed to Cyril of Jerusalem. English translation available in St. Cyril of Jerusalem, *Lectures on the Christian Sacraments,* ed. F. L. Cross (Crestwood, N.Y.: St. Vladimir's Seminary Press, 1986).

4. Chauvet, 260.

5. Chauvet, 446.

6. See the *Catechism of the Catholic Church,* #1099–1103.

7. Nathan Mitchell, "Table Grace," *Assembly* 22:2 (May 1996): 711.

8. Bishops' Committee on the Liturgy, National Conference of *Catholic Bishops, Catholic Household Blessings and Prayers* (Washington, D.C.: United States Catholic Conference, 1989).

9. See M. Skelley, *The Liturgy of the World: Karl Rahner's Theology of Worship* (Collegeville: Liturgical Press, 1991), 92–105. On the cultural challenges to the need to reconnect our daily and sacramental lives, see Michael A. Cowan, "Sacramental Moments: Appreciative Awareness in the Iron Cage," in *Alternative Futures for Worship,* volume 1, ed. R. Duffy (Collegeville: Liturgical Press, 1987), 35–61.

10. See the insightful reflections of J-Glenn Murray, "The Remembering Community," *Plenty Good Room* 3:2 (1995): 2–9. For a discussion of the pervading forces the seem to undermine authentic corporate worship, see Mark Searle, "Private Religion, Individualistic Society, and Common Worship," in *Liturgy and Spirituality in Context: Perspectives on Prayer and Culture,* ed. E. Bernstein (Collegeville: Liturgical Press, 1990), 27–46.

11. Mary Collins, *Contemplative Participation: Sacrosanctum Concilium Twenty-five Years Later* (Collegeville: Liturgical Press, 1990), 82.

12. On ritual as a way of coming to know, see T. Jennings, "On Ritual Knowledge," *The Journal of Religion* 62 (1982): 111–127.

13. R. Hovda, "The Vesting of Liturgical Ministers," in *The Amen Corner,* ed. J. F. Baldovin (Collegeville: Liturgical Press, 1994), 220.

14. The classic presentation is by Y. M.-J. Congar, "L'«ecclesia» ou communauté chrétienne, sujet intégral de l'action liturgique," in *La Liturgie après Vatican II,* ed. J.-P. Jossua (Paris: 1967), 241–282. Also, see A. Nocent, "The Local Church as Realization of the Church of Christ and Subject of the Eucharist," in *The Reception of Vatican II,* ed. G. Alberigo, J.-P. Jossua, and J. Komonchak (Washington, D.C.: Catholic University of America Press, 1987), 215–232.

15. See L. Maldonado, "Liturgy as Communal Enterprise," in *The Reception of Vatican II,* 309–321, esp. 315.

16. Collins, 83.

17. See *Lumen gentium*, 18–29.

18. L. Deiss, *Visions of Liturgy and Music for a New Century* (Collegeville: Liturgical Press, 1996), 29.

19. G. Lathrop, "Thanksgiving at the Holy Table," *WorshipNet* 5 (February 1995): 2.

20. Ralph A. Keifer, *To Give Thanks and Praise: General Instruction of the Roman Missal* (Washington, D.C.: Pastoral Press, 1980), 140.

21. Hovda, 218.

22. Mary Collins, "The Daily Prayer of the Catholic People" (paper presented at the Study Day on Catholic Prayer, "Pray with the Church, Pray as the Church," Washington, D.C., 5 October 1996).

23. *Notitiae* 14 (1978): 300–301, no. 1. I am grateful to Jerome Hall, SJ, for calling my attention to this reply.

24. J. K. Leonard and N. Mitchell, *The Postures of the Assembly during the Eucharistic Prayer* (Chicago: Liturgy Training Publications, 1994), 75.

25. See the Appendix to the *General Instruction of the Roman Missal* for the Dioceses of the United States,#21.

26. J. Huels, *More Disputed Questions in the Liturgy* (Chicago: Liturgy Training Publications, 1996), 22.

27. Huels, 23.

28. John Baldovin, "An Embodied Eucharistic Prayer," introduction to Leonard and Mitchell, 10.

29. Annie Dillard, *Teaching a Stone to Talk* (New York: HarperPerrenial, 1988), 38.

30. A. Kavanagh, *Elements of Rite* (New York: Pueblo, 1982), 15. The context of Kavanagh's observation is a discussion of liturgical environment.

31. E. Foley and M. McGann, *Music and the Eucharistic Prayer* (Collegeville, Minn.: Liturgical Press, 1988), 28. See also *Music in Catholic Worship*, #53–58, in *The Liturgy Documents*, 286–287.

32. See Foley and McGann, 47.

33. See also GIRM, #17, 55b; also the observations of C. Coyne, "Eucharistic Prayers for Masses with Children," *Liturgical Ministry* 4 (Summer 1995): 114, n. 22.

34. E. Foley, "Musical Forms, Referential Meaning and Belief," *Worship* 69 (July 1995): 322.

35. Foley, 327.

36. Deiss, 92.

37. Deiss, 90–93.

38. Introduction, no. 7 in DOL 250, #2005.

39. Marty Haugen, *Mass of Creation* (Chicago: GIA Publications, 1984). Gelineau explored these issues in *The Eucharistic Prayer: Praise of the Whole Assembly* (Washington, D.C.: Pastoral Press, 1985). See the very helpful evaluation and classification of Foley and McGann, 27–46.

40. Action taken by the Bishops' Committee on the Liturgy, communicated in a letter to the author, 7 February 1997.

41. See T. Talley, "Eucharistic Prayers," 16–18. I thoroughly agree with Talley's judgment that the memorial acclamation of the Roman prayers is poorly positioned. Perhaps eventually the pastors of the church will put it after the anamnesis of the prayer, not the supper narrative.

42. R. K. Seasoltz, "Non-verbal Symbols and the Eucharistic Prayer," in Senn, 215.

43. See GIRM, #12. The *Bishops' Committee on the Liturgy Newsletter* (October 1980), commenting on *Inaestimabile Donum*, #6 argues against the use of any instrumental music under the recited prayer.

44. Mary Collins, "The Daily Prayer of the Catholic People."

45. *The Rule of St. Benedict*, ed. T. Fry (Collegeville: Liturgical Press, 1981), prol. 1.

THE PRESIDER'S ROLE

Even with the fullest participation of the assembly, there would be no eucharistic prayer without the presider. The indispensable leadership role of the priest, as we have seen, makes the eucharistic prayer an act of the church, the Body of Christ, head and members. As the "high point of the whole celebration," the eucharistic prayer is "of first importance" among the texts assigned to the presider.[1] Even with the fullest participation of the assembly, "no other single factor affects the liturgy as much as the attitude, style and bearing of the [priest-]celebrant."[2] Thus the presider's role is crucial to the church's eucharistic praying. The full, conscious and active participation of the assembly must be elicited, supported and directed to the right worship of God by full, conscious and active presiding.

FULL PRESIDING

Praying *the* presidential prayer requires leadership that is constantly striving to develop to its height. It requires presiding that has depth and richness. The place where such presiding begins is in a life of prayer. Somehow, priests must find time to make the church's prayer their own if they expect to be able to lead the church in prayer.

But intimately bound to this preparation in prayer must be preparation in action. To lead the people in prayer, one must know how and what they are praying. To invite people to this table, one must invite them daily to communion with each other. To call on them to lift their hearts, one must be acutely aware of what weighs them down. Presiders who have made the joys and sorrows and the longing and aching of the world their own can authentically call the assembly to prayer, name God and the ways God acts, and call the Spirit to fill what is empty.

Presiding with depth and richness takes shape over time. Presiders must be willing to constantly evaluate their growth. People often take stock of themselves spiritually, financially and physically. Presiders must take stock with regard to their leadership of the assembly's prayer. Remembering that we worship a God who casts down the mighty and scatters the proud, presiders should be willing to evaluate their skills periodically by means of videotape and consultation. Yearly reading and rereading of the introductions *(praenotanda)* to the various ritual books and the *General Instruction of the Roman Missal* should become a matter of course. So, too, the act of presiding at liturgy must itself be a priority. If it is just one of the many things that the priest does, the assembly's worship will rarely rise above the mediocre. If presiding is the first thing, the summit and source, of what the priest does, then the assembly's prayer will be rich indeed.

Full presiding means embodying the paradox of being a presider: being simultaneously in the foreground and in the background.[3] Being in the foreground entails being attentive to the ritual action, facilitating the

Attitudes of the Presider and Assembly

Priest-presiders need to accept fully—in their hearts as well as minds—that the eucharistic prayer is the prayer of the whole local church, the laity as well as themselves. Enabling the full participation of everyone in the eucharistic prayer needs to be seen as one of the greatest privileges and opportunities of priests, as well as one of their greatest challenges.

Lay people need to be told on every possible occasion that the eucharistic prayer is their prayer, too. They need to be informed that in the mind of the church it is the center and high point of the entire eucharistic celebration; it is the place in which their fullest participation is not only possible, but needed. They need to accept this fully in their hearts as well as minds.

Excerpts from J. Frank Henderson in National Bulletin on Liturgy, *vol. 24, no. 124 (1991). Copyright © Concacan Inc. All rights reserved. Used by permission of the Canadian Conference of Catholic Bishops, Ottawa, Canada.*

The union of the entire people of God, presbyter and faithful, in the eucharistic celebration must be something that the presider is convinced of in mind and also deep in the heart.

other ministers' roles, choosing every word with extreme care, keeping eye contact with the assembly and being constantly aware of one's demeanor. But this does not translate into the focus of liturgy being on the presider. Rather, "the genius of public worship is the pervasive (in every single thing we say or do in a rite) and clear (in every movement, gesture, word) acknowledgment that we are dealing with a mysterious presence in and beyond us all. We are 'before God.'"[4] Thus the presider is in the background; the chief celebrant of any liturgy is Christ in the Spirit. All the presider says and does must be done with such depth that it leads the assembly to God through Christ in the Spirit. The eucharistic prayer is exactly what its name says it is — prayer.

CONSCIOUS PRESIDING

To voice the assembly's prayer requires conscious presiding. Presiders must ask themselves repeatedly, "What is it that I think I am doing?"

Each answer to that question must repeatedly be measured by the canon of the church's eucharistic prayer.

"Conscious" presiders remember that they draw the "diversity of humanity into the one prayer, the one action, the one communion, which is that of the Body of Christ in the Spirit."[5] They express in their role how the church and Christ are united together in the great prayer of thanksgiving. Young and old, rich and poor, woman and man, sick and sound—the Spirit graces the communion, and Christ prays in and through the local church gathered. The faithful "give thanks to the Father, and offer . . . not only through the hands of the priest but also together with [the priest]" (GIRM, 62). This union of the entire people of God, presbyter and faithful, in the eucharistic celebration must be something that the presider is convinced of in mind and also deep in the heart.[6]

What the presider leads is public, and it is prayer. Therefore, presiders should know the eucharistic prayer and the preface selected by heart and use the sacramentary only as a help to memory. This is public prayer, which requires that the presider has mastered the skills of public proclamation and has internalized this role as the voice of the Body gathered. Singing or speaking, the voice of the presider incarnates the assembly's prayer.

Presiders must know and care for their voices, not for virtuosic performance or personal whim, but to join well the assembly's prayer to Christ's song of praise to the Father, a song of love beyond all telling. Presiders who do not sing at all should proclaim the eucharistic prayer with great care, ensuring that the impact of the words is felt, attending to the different styles of the prayer, avoiding "on the one hand, a monotonous, uninflected style and, on the other, a style of speech and actions too personal and dramatic."[7] Whether singing or speaking, the presider "helps those taking part to form a true community that celebrates and lives out the memorial of the Lord."[8]

The conscious presider respects the church's prayer. It is neither a Sunday morning monologue nor something to be rushed through breathlessly. It is not the presider's prayer—it is the church's prayer. It is not the presider's time—it is God's intersection with human time. The conscious presider prays the texts as they are handed on in the sacramentary: There is no need to intersperse additional words, combine the words of one prayer with another, change the prayer around or use an unapproved text. The presider is not a private person praying. The local gathered assembly, the whole church, which is the Spirit-filled Body of Christ, is praying. The assembly assents with its Amen and has a right that this prayer be the prayer of the church.[9]

Ultimately, the conscious presider is sensitive to style and to the flow of ritual in liturgy. Good style is action that is "appropriate, honest, authentic, as real and genuine as it can be. Good style is acting consciously and humanly and with grace in every living moment."[10] It is not put on and taken off with the chasuble. Every movement of the liturgy, every word spoken, every posture assumed, every object touched is crucial to the whole celebration. And the order of the liturgy — its ritual flow — focuses space and time and moves all toward transformation.

In this age of the informal and chatty, the laid-back and easy, many perceive ritual negatively. Many presiders act embarrassed by ritual or "allergic to liturgy."[11] Everything formal is considered fake, stiff or pompous. Such presiders think that people will feel more at ease if they themselves are casual. But quite the opposite is true. As a sacramental people of the God who took flesh, we take bread, wine, water, oil, touch, sound and bodily movement into our ritual action. They become "breathing spaces that help us discover" who we are and what possibilities our life in God offers.[12] That presence of the Holy One should not make us feel comfortable but should stir us to our core.

The conscious presider knows that treating the symbols and gestures of the liturgy with carelessness and disregard or as strange otherworldly artifacts endangers the assembly's identity. The Holy One comes not as something foreign to us. The presence of the holy can be brought to awareness and communicated to us "only through media which are as we are": creaturely.[13] A conscious presider is also aware that the formal words, gestures and order of the liturgy, especially in the highly formal moment of the eucharistic prayer, are crucial to the assembly's appropriation of the mystery being celebrated.

ACTIVE PRESIDING

To encourage being an active presider may seem to be stating the obvious. But what is at stake is that the presider effectively and actively engage the tools for presiding well: eyes, hands, posture, gesture, voice and the elements of the liturgy that allow for local adaptation. Actively presiding at the eucharistic prayer must enflesh the dynamics of eucharistic praying, confirm the words of the prayer and reverence the Body of Christ on and at the altar-table.

EXHORTATION The active presider taps into the power of the exhortation, or bidding. Exhortations, or "introductions," "are ways of leading the faithful to a more thorough grasp of the meaning of the sacred rites or certain of their parts and to an inner participation in them."[14] The presider is authorized to give an introduction before the beginning of the dialogue of the eucharistic prayer (GIRM, 11). This is a powerful tool, and it must be used very carefully. It is designed to point out to the people thanksgiving themes. This is done in a way best suited to the actual assembly, so that the community may come to perceive the connection between its own life and the history of salvation and may derive greater benefit from celebrating the eucharist.[15]

The exhortation is not a mini sermon. It must be short, adapted to the assembly, poetic and prepared before the liturgy begins. Through the exhortation the presider can link the assembly, its struggle to live, its motives for thanksgiving and its groping to discern the action of God with the ritual act of praying the eucharistic prayer. The exhortation can focus the assembly to see that the prayer gathers together all of their prayer spoken and unspoken, that eucharist is the center and the source of their Christian life. This means that the presider knows the goings-on of the assembly, has witnessed its joy and pain, can name its sin, grace and hope, and can discern ways that God is acting in astonishing ways. Exhortations should draw from the readings and antiphons of the day, be sensitive to the liturgical season and look to the prayer that follows. Good exhortations might resemble the following.

ADVENT III, YEAR B, PREFACE OF ADVENT II

St. Paul enjoins us to rejoice in the Lord and never to cease to render thanks. For the Lord is near to us in an outstretched hand, in the embrace of a friend, in his Body and Blood, the foretaste of the feast to come. Standing watchful and eager for the day Jesus will come again, let us tell the wonder that fills our hearts and call on God to send the Spirit, who makes all things new.

EASTER V, YEAR A, PREFACE OF EASTER II

We are a chosen race, a royal priesthood, a holy nation set apart to proclaim from the rising of the sun to its going down the wonders God has done for us in Jesus. And what wonders they are! Even in the midst of sin and death, God has raised us to new life in Jesus' resurrection. As we continue our 50 days of feasting, let us be very thankful indeed.

SUNDAY XVI OF ORDINARY TIME, YEAR C

We bring our week of work and rest, of surprise visits and unexpected news, our marvel at these summer days and cool nights. Like Martha, let us be attentive and listen to the incomparable things God has done for us. Like Abraham, let us come to a table of rich fare to welcome the Lord of astonishment. Let us come with grateful hearts to give thanks to God, who has made known to us the riches of Christ, our glory and our hope.

Exhortations must be prepared beforehand if they are to be effective and must use words and images that lift the assembly, not bore it with more wordiness. A "well-trained tongue" (see Isaiah 50:4) is crucial to effective exhortations. To work well, the exhortations must never be chatty or breezy or sound like a random listing of personal concerns. The words are brief but deep; the rhetorical effect is to stir the hearers to action. The three or four concrete motives and images for thanksgiving should move into an imperative, "Let us . . . ," that calls all to eucharistic prayer. If the assembly is bidden to gather around the table for the prayer, the exhortation could call them forth in its final line. For example, "As we continue our fifty days of feasting, let us come to the table of the Lord. Gather about and be very thankful indeed." When everyone is in place, the silence would mark the movement into the prayer itself.

SILENCE A crucial tool that the active presider would take up is silence. The eucharistic prayer should be set off from the preparation of the gifts with at least fifteen seconds of silence. This might fall in one of two places. If the assembly remains in the pews, at the conclusion of the prayer over the gifts the presider would join hands and bow the head slightly to observe the silence. If the assembly gathers at the table after the prayer over the gifts, the silence would best fall after all have gathered around. During the silence, nothing else goes on—no page turning, no music arranging, no last-minute minister hustling into place.

VOICE Because the eucharistic prayer to God is an act of public proclamation, the active presider uses basic communication techniques. Any public speaker, no matter how seasoned, needs constantly to remember to speak slowly and clearly. Even if speakers think their speed is just right, it is probably too fast. Microphones pick up what one puts into them: They do not amplify a soft voice, and they capture loudness to the detriment of words. No matter how well the eucharistic prayers are known, the active presider takes time to rehearse them aloud, paying careful attention to pacing and articulation. The prayer is a unified whole, but the subtle moves in the prayer must be captured by close attention to the transitions, which can often be "and" or "who" or "therefore." No one movement of the prayer should be overly extended or emphasized by changing pace or volume.

GESTURE The active presider uses full, meaningful gestures that flow from the act of praying. The sacramentary prescribes that during "The Lord be with you" the presider extends the hands. This should be a full and deliberate motion. Then the presider lifts up the hands: "Lift up your hearts." This gesture should make the assembly feel as if they have been raised up on their toes. Then slowly and deliberately, the presider extends the hands

Gesture and the Eucharistic Prayer

These comments are based on the dream and desire of one dedicated to the *lex orandi*, one who allows this principle to nourish and form his approach, knowing full well that a possible solution to this question remains rather tentative and far from definitive. I make my proposals in the form of rhetorical questions.

Is it possible that one day the Latin church will restore to the institution narrative the same unity, coherence, and uniformity that it enjoyed in the celebrative practice of the first millennium?

The genuflection that the celebrant makes after each consecration, the elevation of the Sacred Species, and the other special signs of adoration still used—do these not isolate and dislocate the institution narrative from its integral relationship to the other elements of the eucharistic prayer?

Are these signs of adoration dependent on an understanding of the mystery of the real presence that reduces it to something static? Might they lead us to consider real presence solely as "being in itself," neglecting that it is also "being for us"?

Is it possible that one day, having developed in a more determined way an active/sacramental understanding of the eucharistic celebration, the Latin church will manage to leave behind the custom advanced by a young bishop of Paris, Odo of Sully, who in the twelfth century introduced the elevation of the consecrated host, to which was subsequently added the elevation of the chalice? . . . And likewise will the Latin church make an enlightened about face with respect to the practice of the genuflection of the celebrant after each consecration, introduced in the fourteenth century?[1]

Every consideration of the literary origin of the eucharistic prayer makes us recall that the gestures made by the celebrating minister that accompany the narrative are not original. The spoken narrative is original. . . . Attention to the literary-theological structure of the eucharistic prayer convinces us that the prayer was not built up in successive layers around a preexisting institution narrative, but it was the narrative that was drawn in and inserted in the manner of an embolism (or literary interpolation) in the preexisting prayer, in order to give maximum weight to the fundamental request for our transformation "into one body."[2]

NOTES

1. Thus writes M. Righetti: "It would be erroneous to believe that the genuflections prescribed by the rubrics of the missal of Pius V after the consecration—an act of adoration of the Blessed Sacrament present on the altar—are original gestures. As far as the celebrant is concerned, up until the fourteenth century the eucharist was adored with a simple bow of the head. As *Ordo* Romanus I says, "The pope, with head bowed, adores the *sancta*." *Ordo Romanus* XIV is the first to have a rubric in this regard after the consecration, but only to direct the celebrant to bow: *inclinato paululum capite* [with head bowed a little]. *(Manuale di storia liturgica*, vol 3 [Ancora, Milano 1966] , 432–433).

2. On the origins of the institution narrative in the eucharistic prayer, see C. Giraudo, *Eucaristia per la chiesa. Prospettive teologiche sull'eucaristia a partire dalla «lex orandi»*, Aloisiana 22 (Brescia and Rome: Morcelliana and Gregorian University Press, 1989), 329–359.

Excerpts from Cesare Giraudo, "Preghiere eucaristiche per la Chiesa di oggi: Riflessioni in margine al commento del canone svizzero-romano," Aloisiana 23 (Rome and Brescia: Gregorian Univeristy Press and Morcelliana, 1993), pp. 108–111. © 1993 Morcelliana and Gregorian University Press. Used with permission. Translated by R. E. McCarron.

in the prayer position, orans, and announces, "Let us give thanks to the Lord our God."

The dialogue is spoken directly to the assembly. The calls and their responses are vital; the presider must be convinced that the people's responses are important and so waits for them before going on, never jumping on the heels of a response.

Once the assembly has responded, the rest of the text is directed to God. While some eye contact with the assembly should be maintained, the presider is not speaking to them but is taking up their prayer. The hands stay in the prayer position until the presider draws them together at the last line of the preface. Then with hands together, the presider joins to sing the Holy, Holy. After the Holy, Holy, the presider extends the hands in orans once more. Later, with palms facing down over the bread and wine, the presider begins the first invocation of the Holy Spirit. The presider closes the hands together, draws them into the chest, reaches out with both hands in the sign of blessing, then brings the hands together again. The movement should communicate invocation. Presiders should

To Mimic Says Too Little

The president of the assembly is not a mimic whose task is to reproduce the Last Supper. The presider is a servant who serves the assembly in its celebration of the eucharist by proclaiming in its midst the motives for which it gives thanks. That on the night before he died, Jesus took bread, said the blessing, broke and gave it to his friends is a central motive for the assembly's giving thanks to God, but, as the eucharistic prayer itself makes clear, it is not the only one. The eucharist is not a mnemonic tableau of an historical event. It is a sweeping thanksgiving for the whole of the Father's benevolence toward the world and this people in Christ and the Holy Spirit. It does no more than what Jesus did in all the meals he took with those he loved. What he did at those meals quite escaped the bounds of any one meal on any one occasion. What he did was to make human beings free and forgiven table partners with God. Mimicking the details of what Jesus did at only one of those meals thus historicizes a mystery which transcends time and place, saying in the process far too little rather than too much. Christian liturgy is not a historical pageant.

Excerpts from Aidan Kavanagh, Elements of Rite *(Collegeville: The Liturgical Press, 1982), pp. 74–75. © 1982 Liturgical Press. Used with permission.*

also be sensitive to the scale of the building. A chapel with ten people gathered calls for more restrained gestures, while a cathedral with thousands might call for more expansive gestures.

The Institution narrative that follows is still part of the prayer to God, and the gesture must flow from the words *as prayer*. The narrative is not dramatic mimicking or play-acting. Thus the gestures called for by the sacramentary must be respected, not elaborated into a *tableau vivant*. The following gestures are prescribed: As the narrative begins, the bread is raised "a little above the altar," not up in the air, not in front of one's face. A slight bow is made as the section "Take this . . ." begins. This slight bow is the only motion prescribed. After "given up for you," the presider "shows the consecrated host to the people," lifting it to chest height. After this "elevation," the presider genuflects. The same execution of gesture follows for the cup.[16] Some presiders have devised elaborate ceremonial and elevate the host and chalice respectively over their heads, turning the body in half-circles. It should be clear that the Order of Mass in the sacramentary, the way the Roman church sets out its prayer, does not prescribe this choreography.

The deacon or presider gives the lead into the acclamation, which the presider sings with all the assembly. At its conclusion, the presider extends the hands in orans for the rest of the prayer to the transition to the final doxology. Again, this is prayer addressed to God, but eyes and bearing must communicate that it is the prayer of both the assembly and presider joined as the Body of Christ. At the final line, the presider brings the hands together, takes the cup and plate (the deacon takes the cup), and here lifts them up at least to head height. The gesture is not showing, as at the Supper narrative, but is an elevation, or offering. The presider alone sings the doxology with the cup and plate elevated. The assembly alone respond with the Amen, and the cup and plate remain elevated until the people have finished their assent. Cup and plate are then placed slowly and gently on the altar. A pronounced moment of silence, like the one that marked the transition to the prayer, would here punctuate the move to the communion rite: no movement, no page turning, but a silence of awe at the wonder of our God.

One of the most profound and effective ways to make this presidential prayer the "center and summit" of the liturgy is to solemnize it by singing it. The integrity of the eucharistic prayer demands that the whole prayer

The Doxology

The doxology of the eucharistic prayer is still part of the presidential prayer, and thus should be proclaimed by the presider alone (at concelebrations, the concelebrants may join in, but are not obliged to do so, cf. GIRM, 191). That this section of the eucharistic prayer is the sole domain of the presider was reiterated by the 1980 *Instruction Inaestimabile Donum*, which states (4): "The doxology itself is reserved to the priest." This is preceded a few sentences earlier by the statement, "It is therefore an abuse to have some parts of the eucharistic prayer said by the deacon, by a lower minister or by the faithful." (Cf. also note R37 to GIRM, 191 in DOL–1581) However, in spite of this statement, it is a common practice for some assemblies to join the presider (sometimes at the presider's invitation) in reciting the doxology. Practically, this tends to trivialize the Great Amen to a whisper, yet it does help many in the assembly feel that they are adequately affirming the eucharistic prayer. In addition, at least among the Maronite Rite Catholics from Lebanon, the final phrase of the doxology of the eucharistic prayer ("now and always and forever") is communally recited, indicating that the practice is in the realm of liturgical possibility. In addition, the Maronites also communally recite a doxology during the breaking of the bread which immediately follows the eucharistic prayer and precedes the Lord's Prayer.

Nevertheless, all things being equal, in the Roman rite, the presider should not invite the assembly to join him in reciting the doxology (since it does break up the unity of this presidential prayer), and instead should foster efforts to enhance the Great Amen which follows.

Some scholars have found ancient texts which indicate that this is the high point of the eucharistic prayer — theoretically and physically/visually. This is the major "physical" elevation. This is the point for the visible "offering," the point at which the gesture of offering gifts to heaven found in the Hebrew Scriptures should be imitated. Unfortunately, many presiders are still under the impression that the height prescribed in the Tridentine Missal (a few inches) should be continued now. The contrary is true. Although nothing is specifically mentioned in the sacramentary, evidence suggests that the doxology is the time to the grand gesture of lifting high the gifts toward heaven for all to see.

be sung when at all possible. Yet this is a formidable prescription for the parish whose music ministry is fledgling or under-resourced and whose presiders are less than endowed with a voice for public performance.

We should recognize that the terms "sung prayer" or "singing the prayer" might strike fear into the heart of the less musically inclined presider. While there are more lyrical through-composed settings in a contemporary idiom available for those so gifted, the music set out in the sacramentary and being composed by many contemporary musicians is *recitative* or *cantillation*, a genre of music that falls somewhere between speech and song and in which the musical element is at the service of the words and their rhythm and structure.[17] The music in use for such a setting is like a psalm tone: With conscientious practice, most presiders could easily use these settings for the whole prayer.

In a fine example, tone formulae have been composed that correspond to the keys of the most familiar acclamations.[18] A presider with an adequate voice could learn them quickly; the tone form respects the cadence of the words of the prayer, which we saw is a descendent of the dynamic of the psalms, and the acclamations flow musically by being in the same key as the prayer. The acclamations themselves and their instrumental arrangement add musical interest to prevent the tonal forms from being perceived as overly monotonous.

Presiders with any voice at all should sing the whole prayer; if they do not, they should proclaim the whole prayer. To sing only parts of the prayer creates an imbalance that can rupture the unity of the prayer, even if it has strong musical transitions from spoken to sung to spoken again. A recited preface after a sung dialogue pulls down the spirit of thanksgiving, which should soar. To sing only the Supper narrative unduly sets it off from the epiclesis and anamnesis to which it is ordered.

The active presider recognizes that singing the prayer is significant and seeks to learn and to build confidence. Despite what has been said above about singing the whole prayer, presider and assembly may take a year or more to work up to this. They could begin with the doxology, the final burst of praise of the prayer that logically calls forth song. The presider should never decide alone when lifting the plate and cup that this is the day to sing. Well before Sunday, the music minister and presider should work with the tone that flows into the Amen. They can rehearse so that the presider can find the pitch or know how to take the pitch the music minister gives. Then the transitions to the other acclamations can be practiced: the opening dialogue, the final lines of the preface and the call to the memorial acclamation. Since it is bound to the acclamation that will be used, the presider will need to know. Once comfortable with sustaining pitch, transitions and tempo, the presider can take on the rest of the prayer. At first, the presider might simply chant the prayer *recto tono*, all in the same tone, with the acclamations and carefully placed extra "amens" breaking the possible monotony. "For the sake of the people" the presider must "rehearse carefully the sung parts that contribute to their celebration."[19]

HOMILY AND THE EUCHARISTIC PRAYER

Presiding well at the eucharistic prayer requires preaching well. The homily "is a proclamation of the wonders God works now in our midst. . . . Homiletic preaching is worship."[20] The homilist discerns the activity of God in the people's lives, opens up the scriptures proclaimed and through compelling language enables the community to name the presence of God and live in conformity to the gospel message. In the homily, the preacher gives the assembly a reason to celebrate:

> The preacher is called to point to the signs of God's presence in the lives of the people so that, in joyous recognition of this presence, they may join the angels and saints to proclaim God's glory and sing with them their unending hymn of praise.[21]

If the presider sees the homily not only as an intrinsic part of the liturgy of the word but also as directly ordered to the eucharistic prayer, then the assembly will as well. The similarity in dynamic and content between the homily and the eucharistic prayer will awaken the assembly to the way that the prayer synthesizes the interaction of the memory of God's wonders of old, the Spirit at work in our midst and our hope for the promised day of Jesus' return. So too, if the homily is ordered to the eucharistic prayer, if it is the fruit of the presider's interaction with the assembly during the week, if it is the compelling recall of memories and the call to live the gospel, if it urges the whole assembly (preacher included) to become living sacrifices of praise, then both the homily and the eucharistic prayer will be celebrated as acts of the church's worship, not as the presider's monologue.

The presider's role at the eucharistic prayer is to preside fully, consciously and actively so that the prayer of the assembly may be the prayer of Christ, head and members. While many presiders might breathe a sigh of relief that the church's practice of spontaneous eucharistic praying every Sunday has long passed, bringing life to the eucharistic prayers we have written down today still demands work and prayer. "Giving voice to every creature under heaven" (EP IV) is an awesome task, and all that the presider does in voice, body and life must acclaim God and glorify God's name.

NOTES

1. Pastoral Introduction to the Order of Mass, # 35; GIRM, 10.

2. *Music in Catholic Worship*, # 21.

3. R. Hovda, "Sunday No Better? — After All This Betterment?" in *Robert Hovda: The Amen Corner*, ed. J. F. Baldovin (Collegeville: Liturgical Press, 1994), 145 – 151.

4. Hovda, 148 – 149.

5. D. N. Power "Representing Christ in Community and Sacrament," *Being A Priest Today*, ed. D. Goergen (Collegeville: Liturgical Press, 1992), 121.

6. Cf. Hovda, 3.

7. *Eucharistiae participationem*, Circular Letter of the Sacred Congregation for Divine Worship (April 1973), no. 17; in (DOL 248, # 1991).

8. *Eucharistiae participationem*, 17; in DOL 248, # 1991.

9. Cf. *Eucharistiae participationem*, 11; DOL 248, # 1985.

10. Hovda, *Strong, Loving, and Wise* (Collegeville: Liturgical Press, 1980), 63 – 64.

11. J. F. Baldovin, "Must Eucharist Do Everything?" *liturgical ministry* 1 (Summer 1992): 99 – 100.

12. Nathan Mitchell, "Symbols Are Actions, Not Objects — New Directions for an Old Problem," *Living Worship* 13:2 (1977).

13. See L. Gilkey, "Symbols, Meaning, and the Divine Presence," *Theological Studies* 35 (1974): 260.

14. *Eucharistiae participationem*, 14 in DOL 248, # 1988. I am translating the Latin word *monitio* as "exhortation." See also the *Directory for Masses with Children*, 22, which allows for "the insertion of motives for giving thanks" before the dialogue.

15. *Eucharistiae participationem*, 8 in DOL 248, # 1982.

16. For a brief historical survey and a careful examination of current gesture in the context of a theology of the eucharist, see J. F. Baldovin, "*Accepit panem*: The Gestures of the Priest at the Institution Narrative of the Eucharist" in *Rule of Prayer, Rule of Faith: Essays in Honor of Aidan Kavanagh, OSB*, ed. N. Mitchell and J. F. Baldovin (Collegeville: Liturgical Press, 1996), 123 – 139.

17. See Foley and McGann, 28. And M. Veuthey, *Dans vos assemblées*, vol. 1 (Paris: Desclée, 1989), 156.

18. The work is by Robert P. McMurray, staff member of the Office for Pastoral Liturgy, Diocese of Cleveland, Ohio.

19. *Music in Catholic Worship*, # 22.

20. Anthony M. Pilla, *In Times Like These, O God, Let Your Word Rain Down*, Pastoral Letter on Music, 13 September 1996 (Cleveland, Ohio), #31. See also *Eucharistiae participationem*, 15.

21. National Conference of Catholic Bishops, *Fulfilled in Your Hearing: The Homily in the Sunday Assembly*, # 15.

THE PREPARATION OF THE ALTAR AND GIFTS

While our primary concern has been the eucharistic prayer, we need also to be attentive to the entrance into that prayer, or the opening of the "liturgy of the eucharist." We must concern ourselves with the preparation of the altar and the gifts. How can this preparation rite lead us into the central moment of the eucharistic prayer? How can it prepare not only the bread, wine and table but also the celebrants themselves? The sacramentary has very flexible directives here, perhaps more flexible than any other moment in the liturgy. Therefore, each parish must take stock of its cultural, architectural and spiritual resources and transcribe its own choreography for the preparation rites. Our zealous but often misguided crafting of liturgy in the years following the conciliar reform may have led us to devalue or misappropriate this initial movement of the eucharistic liturgy. Its origins are indeed practical and only gradually took on more ceremony. We are right to see that it is not climactic, but this should not lead us to neglect it. Moreover, the nagging influence of the pre–Vatican II "offertory" usage still sways many presiders' execution of the rite.

The sacramentary gives the following elements for the preparation of the altar and gifts: the altar is prepared; the bread and wine, the gifts for the poor and the money collected for the church are brought up by members of the assembly, perhaps accompanied by a song; the presider places the gifts on the altar and then may incense them; the presider washes his hands and then prays the prayer over the gifts to conclude the rite (see GIRM, 49 – 53). How might these elements be orchestrated so that the rite becomes truly a "preparation for the eucharistic prayer" (GIRM, 53)?

What Gifts Do We Bring?

First, we must consider the gifts themselves. The eucharistic prayer is prayed over bread and wine. This poses important questions: What are we using for "bread and wine," and what do we put them in? If we persist in using lily-white little mass-produced hosts pressed flat by professionals, and antique, highly stylized vessels, the assembly will be hard-pressed to see the gifts as their own, as symbols of themselves, of the goodness of creation and the dignity of the human action required to bake bread and make wine. The gifts become so fossilized that their purpose and natural symbolism of God can no longer shine forth.[1]

What do we do with the gifts of bread and wine at the beginning of Mass? Are they in a position of honor that all the assembly can see as they arrive?

We also bring money. In contemporary Western society, money and our collection of it has great importance. While it may seem a "utilitarian and secular interlude, . . . cash offering probably is more vigorously symbolic of a modern assembly's gift of itself."[2] We run giving campaigns, exhort our assemblies to use the envelope system and try to bolster our collections, but what we do ritually with that collection of money can say more than any impassioned speech from the finance committee chair. To collect the money with some dignity says that our act of giving is important and that our gift is a symbol of ourselves, our family and our household's sacrifice. That money is for building up the Body of Christ gathered locally, for the care and maintenance of the house of that church, and for the poor. And if an assembly is convinced of the importance of its act, giving more might seem reasonable, and taking responsibility for building up the church and caring for the poor might be seen as a Christian duty.

That is why some assemblies process forward, with each person or a representative of each family coming up, to place the money in a basket or in some other vessel. Where space or size might preclude such a full procession, the collection needs to be done with care. Safety may require that the collection be locked up as soon as it is taken forward, but let the money be carried with care to where it must go, not be whisked away by an usher. If gifts for the poor are brought as well as money, or are collected with the money, they too can be borne in procession and placed near the table until the end of the liturgy. A regular collection of food or clothing for the poor can make a crucial connection between our eucharist and our work for justice.

Bread, wine, money and gifts for the poor: These are the only gifts that are ever brought in the procession of the gifts. There is absolutely no occasion for which any other things are brought to or are placed on or near the altar. If we cannot see the bread and wine as symbols of ourselves, our community, our lives, if they do not sum up what it means for us to die and live in Christ Jesus, if they do not bespeak the goodness of the earth and our commitment to it, if they do not cry out for us to work for justice, then attention needs to be given to the bread and wine and to preaching.

While the money and gifts are collected, the altar is prepared. The GIRM directs, "Corporal, purificator, missal and chalice are placed on [the altar] (unless the chalice is prepared at a side table)" (49). If we are using substantial vessels and are observing the fraction rite, our handkerchief corporals need to be replaced with a corporal of suitable size that is spread on the table. There is to be one book on the altar. If any music or sheets with text for the interpolations within the eucharistic prayer are needed, these should be carefully placed in a dignified binder so that there are no extraneous papers, music scores or additional books on the altar.

How Do We Handle the Gifts?

The central ritual act is the placing of the one plate of bread and the flagon of wine on the altar itself (GIRM, 49). Those who bring up the gifts need to be reminded of the importance of their action. They are not in a race up the aisle. Let them hold them up and move at a careful pace. There is no reason for the gifts to be "received" away from the table or at the steps

If we cannot see the bread and wine as symbols of ourselves, our community, our lives, then attention needs to be given to the bread and wine and to preaching.

leading to it; the GIRM simply says "at a convenient place." The money might be carried first, and then the bread and wine bearers could come and stand on opposite sides of the altar.

The presider takes the plate, holds it slightly above the table and inaudibly says the prayer. Even if there is no song, these prayers are best said inaudibly. This way, the ritual gesture of placing the gifts remains central, and the minimal use of words heightens the great words of the eucharistic prayer to come. The presider then carefully places the plate on the altar. If there is a deacon, the cup might be prepared at the credence table, in which case the person carrying the flagon of wine would go there first while the deacon mixed the cup. That person would then accompany the deacon, with the prepared cup, to the presider and hand it to him. If there is no deacon, the cup and water are brought by another minister, the wine from the flagon is poured in and mixed, and the presider takes the flagon and cup, holds them slightly above the altar, says the prayer inaudibly, and then places them on the altar. The bread and wine bearers bow and return to their places.

The gifts might then be incensed, especially during the Christmas and Easter seasons and on festive occasions. The censer is swung slowly back and forth three times over the gifts. The incensation must be done "with grave and graceful mein . . . with measured beat," with only the arm moving and the censer held by the top of the chain.[3] The altar is then incensed "with a series of single swings" as the presider walks around it. If there is a cross nearby, it is incensed first, then the altar. If the cross is behind the altar, the presider incenses it when passing in front of it, with three swings back and forth.[4] Then the deacon or an assisting minister takes the censer, bows and incenses the presider with three swings back and forth, and bows again.

A Future Adaptation

The *General Instruction of the Roman Missal* directs that "the faithful's offerings are received by the priest, assisted by the ministers, and put in a suitable place; the bread and wine for the eucharist are taken to the altar" (101). From the moment the gifts arrive at the altar, all of the preparatory prayers and gestures take place there. Are there any possible alternatives to this arrangement which would help to clarify the preparatory nature of the presentation of the gifts? I propose the following. After the general intercessions, the preparation of the gifts and altar begins. While the presider remains standing at the chair, water is brought for the washing of his hands. In our culture this simple gesture at the outset of the presentation of the gifts would certainly seem appropriate and eas-

ily understood, since it is not uncommon to wash one's hands before handling things of worth, especially food stuff which is to be served for eating. . . .

The gifts of bread and wine for the eucharist, along with the gifts for the poor, are then carried to the presider at the presidential chair by representatives of the assembly. (As the celebrant receives the gifts of bread and wine, the other ministers [deacon and/or acolytes] prepare the altar by placing upon it the altar cloth, corporal, purificator, sacramentary and chalice into which some of the wine, when it arrives at the altar, is poured and so readied for the eucharistic prayer. Other vessels and purificators are brought to the altar only during the *fractio*.) The priest accepts the container of bread

Though the incensation of the assembly may seem awkward or lengthy, it should not be omitted if the gifts are incensed. The assembly, the Body of Christ, is reverenced just as the altar and cross, presider and gifts are. Given that the assembly is usually divided into sections, they should be incensed according to section as a body. The assisting minister bows to the assembly and honors them with incense. This also can be done by walking all through the assembly, swinging the censer.

The hands of the presider are washed. This should be a real washing of hands with water poured and a towel used, all done in the sight of the assembly as a ritual act: It is a symbol of cleansing and preparation of the presider before the holy work of leading the people's prayer.[5] The prayer over the gifts would then be prayed, keeping in mind that the "Pray brothers and sisters" for this prayer is an expanded form of "Let us pray."

At this juncture, some assemblies whose size and liturgical space permit come forward to stand about the altar. Care must be taken

and, holding it in a manner for all to see (slightly extended in front of himself), recites the berakah text: "Blessed are you, Lord . . . we have this bread for the eucharist. . . . It will become for us the bread of life." The bread is handed back to the one who presented it and he or she then continues to process to the altar, where the gift is placed. Meanwhile, the gift of wine is brought to the priest, who adds a small amount of water and then says the berakah prayer: "Blessed are you, Lord . . . we have this wine for the eucharist. . . . It will become our spiritual drink." (Thomas A. Krosnicki, *Mixtio Aquae cum Vino*: A Case Study of Moral Unity," *Ephemerides Liturgicae* [1990]: 182–86. The option to recite the berakah prayers quietly would remain as indicated in the present sacramentary.) The priest hands the flagon of wine back to the gift bearer, who processes to the altar. The gifts for the poor, gathered as the members of the assembly arrive for the eucharist, are received by the priest in a silent gesture of acceptance and then carried in procession by an appropriate minister to be placed near the altar.

The prayer over the gifts serves then as a fitting conclusion to this entire structural unit. When it is concluded, the celebrant, accompanied by the acolytes, processes to the altar where everything has been readied for the liturgy of the eucharist. . . .

Upon arriving at the altar, the celebrant's first words and gestures are those of the opening to the eucharistic prayer—the preface dialogue. The preparation period is over; the great eucharistic prayer begins.

Excerpts from "Preparing the Gifts: Clarifying the Rite," by Thomas A. Krosnicki, SVD. Divine Word Missionaries, Techny, IL 60082. Copyright © 1991. Used with permission. This article appeared in Worship *magazine, vol. 65 (1991), pp. 154–157.*

that this is done with solemnity, movement and joy. The presider could give the exhortation that leads into a call to the assembly to come forward. Ushers or other ministers might then lead the assembly forward. All bow to the altar and then move around the table. After a moment of silence, the presider begins the dialogue. While parishes that have a full procession of the assembly at the preparation of the gifts might decide to have the assembly move around the table as part of the preparation, the distinct mark and shift in posture at the beginning of the eucharistic prayer itself, might be more desirable. The bringing of gifts to the altar, and the joyful march of the people "who approach the altar in hopeful expectation"[6] to offer together the sacrifice of praise, might be seen as two distinct movements or made into one. However, too much movement at this time could do more to distract from the prayer than to foster it. At any rate, a solemn moment of silence and stillness would be observed and then the prayer begun.

How might a preparation of the gifts be orchestrated then, taking seriously what has been set out here from the rite? The following are three patterns that have been adapted by parishes that have sought to recover the dignity and importance of the first movement of the liturgy of the eucharist—taking gifts.[7] All of them allow for the preparation rite to end and the eucharistic prayer to have a clear beginning.

A Place to Start

The ushers begin to pass the baskets while the servers place the book and empty cup on the altar. On occasion, a song may be sung by all. At other times, a choral selection or instrumental music might be used.

Two members of the assembly bring forward the bread and wine, and an usher brings forward the basket with all the collected money. Each holds the gifts slightly away from the body and up. The presider comes to the table as they all move forward and acknowledges the money as the usher presents it. The usher then takes it to the safe in a dignified way. Then the bread- and winebearers come forward. The presider takes the plate and, holding it slightly above the table, prays the prayer quietly and places the plate on the altar. The presider then takes the cup, pours in the wine and water, takes the wine and cup, and, holding them slightly above the table, pauses for the prayer, then sets them down. The gift bearers bow and return to their places. The servers bring the pitcher of water, large bowl and towel, and they wash the presider's hands. The prayer over the gifts with its invitation is prayed with the assembly still seated.

A pause of stillness and quiet is observed, and then the exhortation for the eucharistic prayer is given.

COME WITH JOY TO THE COURTS OF THE LORD: EXPANDING THE PROCESSION

The presider stands and comes to the front of the assembly and gives the bidding:

> Sisters and brothers, the apostle Paul appeals, "By the mercies of God, present yourselves as a living sacrifice, holy and acceptable to God, which is your spiritual worship." Come, then, present yourself with your gifts of bread and wine: work of your hands and harvest of the earth. Come then with your gift of money: fruit of your labor and pledge of your dedication. Come then with your gifts for the poor: a hand stretched out to the hungry and a cover against the cold. Let us make good on our vow to the Most High.

All stand. As the presider and acolytes go to the back of the room, the choir begins a song in which everyone can participate through the refrain.

The procession begins from the back of the room. First come two adults holding bowls of billowing incense. They process to the front, with the bowls held out in front of them, and stand at the head of the center aisle, facing the approaching procession. The presider and minister fall in behind, and the people from the back begin moving forward behind them. The presider, and then all the others, come to the incense bearers, turn toward one of them, reach out an open palm and draw the smoke of the incense to themselves, breathing it in or making the sign of the cross. Each person bows deeply to the altar and places offerings in the baskets—

one for the money and one for the gifts for the poor. Like everyone else, the presider too makes an offering. Even if unable to make a monetary offering (or if making an offering at the end of the month), members would still come up to present themselves with a deep bow. Ushers very kindly assist as the people come forward. People move in time to the music; they return to their places and remain standing, singing the refrain.

The last people in the procession carry the plate of bread and flagon of wine, both lifted up with great dignity. One incense bearer moves in front of them and leads the giftbearers to the table; the other follows behind. They process to the table and stand on either side, reverently holding the gifts. The incense bowls are placed on the floor, near the table.

The presider approaches the table, takes the bread and then places it on the table. Meanwhile, the cup and water are brought over, the cup is poured and mixed, and the presider places the flagon and cup on the

Preparation as Quiet Anticipation

See also "A Future Adaptation" (page 122), a beginning point for a parish's further ordering of the preparation rite.

■ After the intercessions, the assembly is seated and the presider goes to meet the ushers with their baskets and the gift bearers with the bread and wine, somewhere in the midst of the assembly, toward the altar. They gather together, and the presider, speaking to the whole assembly, says:

Pray, sisters and brothers, that the gifts we bring for the poor and for the church, today and every day, may with this bread and wine be acceptable to God our almighty Father.

The assembly responds as usual.

■ The ushers begin the collection, and the gift bearers go to the table, where they place the bread and wine. The one carrying the flagon pours wine into the chalice. They then return to their places in the assembly. Acolytes have placed the cup and book on the table. The presider does not spend time at the table but goes to the chair. Acolytes come there to wash the presider's hands, and the presider sits.

■ When the collection has been completed and the song (if there is one) is also finished, the presider, still sitting, prays the prayer over the gifts. This is done very quietly. All respond, "Amen."

■ The presider stands and gestures for all to do so. The presider then walks to the table, and all from the assembly who wish come and gather there also. The first words spoken at the table then are the dialogue of the eucharistic prayer.

—Gabe Huck

table. The giftbearers bow and go back to their places. The prayer over the gifts with its invitation is prayed.

RECEIVE OUR GIFTS: COMING TO THE WELCOME-TABLE

The nave of the church is in "choir" style. After the intercessions, all are seated as the baskets are passed. There is instrumental music from this time until the dialogue that begins the eucharistic prayer.

When the collection is finished, the presider goes to the table. Two people from the assembly bring the bread and wine, and another brings the collected money. All walk slowly with the gifts held forward. As they approach the table, the bread- and winebearers go to the left and right sides of the altar, and the person carrying the money takes it reverently to the place reserved for it. The bread- and winebearers place the vessels on the table and then stand beside the presider. All three bow deeply. Then the giftbearers return to their places.

The servers bring the censer and incense to the presider, who first honors the gifts and table with incense. As he comes to the assembly, all stand, and he passes through them slowly, honoring them with the incense. All bow as the incense comes before them.

The presider moves back toward the altar-table, and the assembly follows after him. All gather around the altar. The music ends, and the prayer over the gifts is prayed. A long pause is observed, and then the dialogue begins.

NOTES

1. See L.-M. Chauvet, *Symbol and Sacrament: A Sacramental Reinterpretation of Christian Existence,* trans. P. Madigan and A. Beaumont (Collegeville: Liturgical Press, 1995), 330–339; and M. Collins, "Critical Questions for Liturgical Theology," in *Worship Renewal to Practice* (Washington, D.C.: Pastoral Press, 1987), 128–132. See G. Huck, *The Communion Rite at Sunday Mass* (Chicago: Liturgy Training Publications, 1989), for a fuller discussion of bread, wine and vessels.

2. A. Kavanagh, *Elements of Rite* (New York: Pueblo, 1982), 65.

3. The *Ceremonial of Bishops,* 92 and 91, 75.

4. GIRM 235 and *Ceremonial of Bishops,* 93.

5. See F. McManus, "From 1964 to 1969: The Preparation of the Gifts," in *Shaping English Liturgy,* ed. P. Finn and J. Schellman (Washington, D.C.: Pastoral Press, 1990), 132.

6. L. Deiss, *Visions of Liturgy and Music for a New Century* (Collegeville: Liturgical Press, 1996), 149.

7. These second and third examples are adapted from the careful observation and report of Gabe Huck in *Liturgy 90* (January 1994): 14–15.

HOW DO WE GET THERE?

elebrating and praying well the eucharistic prayer at Sunday Mass may seem a formidable task: continual conversion to eucharistic living, careful preparation and full ritual celebration. So where do we begin? The questions on page 129 will help, but it should come as no surprise that the first steps do not involve changes at Sunday liturgy.

FIRST STEP ON THE WAY

To make the eucharistic prayer the center and summit of the Sunday liturgy and thus the center and summit of our Christian lives, we need to focus attention first on those who pray the eucharistic prayer: the members of the assembly. Our focus must be not only on what goes on when the assembly gathers but on cultivating households of thanksgiving. The importance of household ritual, even if it means simply marking morning and evening with the Lord's Prayer or a psalm, can come again and again into the preaching and the bulletin in consistent ways. But the parish can also provide occasion for people to begin to do this well. Putting together a book of prayers will achieve little until a pattern of prayer takes hold in people's prayer lives. Meetings, group gatherings, shared meals and the beginning and end of the day all can be marked in common with a short blessing. In time, the rhythm of blessing God will become natural.

Members of the assembly, too, must commit to marking with thanksgiving their times of eating, particularly the evening meal, even if it is not taken together. Table prayer will always echo eucharistic praying.

Leader: Let us give thanks to the Lord our God!
All: It is right to give our thanks and praise!

Lord, you are holy;
you are the fountain of all holiness.
We give you thanks for your gift of food and drink.
Strengthen us in body and spirit
to be ready to provide for all in need.
We ask this through Christ our Lord.

Checklist: Toward Full Eucharistic Praying

Above all, by taking care to prepare for the prayer and to do the prayer with reverence, dignity and deliberateness, we can learn what eucharistic prayer is about. In light of what has been laid out about the roles and ritual context of the prayer, the following are some points that just about any assembly can seek to implement:

1. Is there a distinct moment of silence to punctuate the move from the prayer over the gifts or the exhortation to the dialogue?

2. Would a carefully composed exhortation help introduce the prayer? Is this exhortation (which need not change week to week but could change with the seasons), the eucharistic prayer itself and whatever music is needed for it in a pleasing book for the presider to use, a book worthy of the text it contains?

3. Which posture is assumed by the assembly? Do they stand around the table having processed to it with their gifts, or do they come forward after the prayer over the gifts? If space precludes their standing about the table, does the assembly stand or kneel aright?

4. Has the presider carefully prepared the preface and prayer for public proclamation? Has the presider rehearsed the gestures indicated by the sacramentary? Is the presider given feedback on pace, tone of voice, posture, eyes, hands?

5. Are the transitions to the acclamations smooth? Are they all of the same setting? Is the music suitable for the act of acclamation? Do music ministers, presider and assembly respect their roles?

6. Is it clear that the Supper narrative is part of the prayer? Are the gestures only those called for by the sacramentary?

7. Are the gifts raised at the doxology, which is said or sung by the presider alone? Do they remain elevated during the whole Amen?

8. Does a distinct moment of silence punctuate the transition from the eucharistic prayer to the communion rite?

9. Is the parish baking bread for every Sunday eucharist? Is the cup always offered, and has consistent catechesis meant that it is taken by an ever-growing number?

This simple grace will draw attention not only to the act of praying grace before meals but subtly to the fact that all our food and drink is a gift from God. So, also, taking up the language of thanksgiving will shape our way of praying. As households become used to prayer at the beginning of meals, longer forms or some scripture can be incorporated, especially on special occasions. The presence of some good bread and wine on the table on special occasions could recall strongly for us that "every morsel of bread is the product and result of an entire history" of death and life and that wine "gives rise to joy and merriment."[1] This simple formation through household ritual and prayer can shape the eucharistic spirituality demanded to pray well the eucharistic prayer at liturgy.

LITURGICAL LIFE OF THE PARISH

With the groundwork for prayer laid at home, parish leadership can evaluate the types of liturgical prayer in the community outside the Sunday eucharist. A sorely neglected form of prayer in our treasury is blessing: blessing of persons, buildings and human activity, blessing of devotional articles, blessings related to feasts and seasons, and blessings for various needs and occasions. Through the celebration of blessings, the "faithful receive the wisdom to discern the reflections of God's goodness not only in the elements of creation but also in the events of human life."[2]

These blessings are intimately linked to the celebration of the eucharist and communion, for it is from the eucharist itself that the church becomes a blessing to the world (*Book of Blessings*, 8). The blessings themselves exemplify the rule of eucharistic praying: "A blessing consists of two parts: first, the proclamation of the word of God, and second, the praise of God's goodness and the petition for God's help" (20). Anything that a community does to foster reverence and appreciation for the gift of creation and time, the ability of created things and human activity to reveal the presence of God in our midst, will strengthen a parish's eucharistic prayer.

If a parish wishes to shape an assembly that prays the eucharistic prayer well, regular celebration of the Liturgy of the Hours can make a dif-

Our focus must be not only on what goes on when the assembly gathers but on cultivating households of thanksgiving.

ference. The Liturgy of the Hours itself is the daily celebration of the pasch of Christ in the rhythms of the morning and evening. The office draws on the psalms, whose thanksgiving, lament, supplication and vow of praise are at the roots of our eucharistic prayer. Even if the times or other constraints of our gathering preclude a full celebration of the Hours, a simplified form with opening verse, psalm and prayer could take shape. What will begin to happen is a commitment to the prayer life of the parish and to a eucharistic spirituality. This simply means that instead of isolating the Sunday eucharist, we have begun to let it give flavor and direction to our ritual and to our lives.

Parish leadership needs to step back and evaluate how the assembly is celebrating and then challenge what is lacking, repair what is broken and move forward to what is better. This will require careful education for both assembly and ministers.

Using the Preliminary Gathering for Catechesis

When a parish is serious about improving its Sunday liturgy, and particularly the eucharistic prayer, catechesis for the whole assembly is needed, but difficult. Adult education sessions draw only a small portion of the assembly. Here are some alternatives.

Formation for the celebration of the eucharistic prayer might take place in a "preliminary gathering" at the Sunday eucharist during one season or over a period of weeks. The notion of a preliminary gathering grows out of the tradition of fellowship and witnessing in the African American religious tradition.[3] The preliminary gathering has been effective in many African American parishes where a deacon or lay minister or, in their absence, the presider builds up community and expresses the presence of Christ in the gathering. Though not used primarily to catechize, it seems quite effective when the catechesis relates to the liturgy that is to be celebrated. The rest of the church can draw on the gifts these parishes offer.

The instruction itself occurs in the context of prayer and is directly related to the liturgy. It should not be more than 10 to 15 minutes long. Here is an example:

- An instrumental prelude as the assembly gathers

- A scriptural greeting and introduction

When all have gathered, the minister who will lead greets the assembly. "Good Morning" and the like are never appropriate greetings of the Body of Christ assembled. The words are to be taken from scripture or scriptural images and should be drawn from the liturgical feast. The Book of Blessings, *the invitatories of the Liturgy of the Hours and the entrance or responsorial psalm refrains provide many examples. For example, a lay minister might say throughout the year on Sunday:*

> Saints of God! Let us bless God who does all things wisely, let us praise God who lifts up the lowly and fills us with breath to sing praise and thanks!
> All: Blessed be God forever (or Amen)!

or

Leader: Sisters and brothers, come let us draw near to the God who saves us, and worship the Lord who has done great things for us!

All: Blessed be God forever (or Amen)!

■ Catechesis

The leader then moves to instruction on the specific aspect of the eucharistic prayer. An introduction can contextualize the instruction.

Leader: Blessed is God indeed, the One who has gathered us together this morning in the Holy Spirit, who helps us to pray as we ought. And that we might pray well before the Lord who made us, that we might worship the Lord wisely with our hearts and minds and voices, we need to be aware of what we do. When we come before the altar to pray the eucharistic prayer, we begin with a dialogue. . . .

■ Prayer and Greeting

At the conclusion of the instruction, the leader then calls the assembly to a brief prayer and ritual expression of community:

Leader: Our God blesses us with mercy and strengthens us with love. Our God gathers us together, the whole and the broken, the rejoicing and the mourning, the lonely and the loved, the saint and the sinner. Let us ask God to knit our community up in the unity of the Spirit.

(Pause for prayer.)

Good and gracious God, once more you have brought us this day to stand before you on holy ground. Come by here, Lord, and rouse us to recognize you in our sisters and brothers at our side. Build us up where we are broken down, and set us aflame with your Spirit that we may worthily magnify your great Name: you, one God, Father, Son and Holy Spirit, now and forever.

All: Amen!

Leader: Let us greet one another in the Spirit of love.

As the assembly exchanges welcomes, the music for the opening hymn is played underneath. When the procession and assembly are in place, the hymn begins.

Each week, a part of the eucharistic prayer or a different aspect of what praying the eucharistic prayer means might be expounded. Then the specific aspects of active participation can be taken up, like singing or posture. Further sessions could then take up the preparation of the gifts or communion.

Preaching from the Eucharistic Prayer

Hear, then, briefly, what the apostle, or, better, what Christ says by the mouth of the apostle, concerning the sacrament of the Lord's table: "We, though many, are one bread, one body" (1 Corinthians 10:17). That is all there is to it, as I have quickly summed it up. Yet do not count the words, but rather, weigh their meaning. For if you count them, they are few, but if you ponder them, their import is great. "One bread," he said. No matter how many loaves were placed on the altar then, there was only one bread. No matter how many loaves are placed upon the altars of Christ throughout the world today, it is but one bread. What is meant by "one bread"? He explained it concisely, "We, though many, are one body." This bread is the Body of Christ to which the apostle refers when he addresses the church: "Now you are the Body of Christ and his members" (1 Corinthians 12:27). What you receive, you yourselves are by the grace by which you have been redeemed. You show agreement when you respond "Amen." What you see here is the sacrament of unity.

The apostle has shown us briefly what this bread is. Now consider the matter carefully and see how it comes about. How is bread made? Wheat is threshed, milled, moistened and baked. By moistening, the wheat is purified, and by baking, it is made firm. What was your threshing? You were made in this way: Your threshing was in fasting, in the lenten observances, in vigils, in exorcisms. You were milled when you were exorcized. But moistening cannot be done without water. Thus you were baptized. Baking is troublesome, but beneficial. What, then, is the baking? The fire of temptations from which no life is free. And how is this beneficial? "The furnace tries the potter's vessel, and the trial of affliction the just" (Sirach 27:6). As one loaf results from combining the individual grains and mixing them together with water, so also the one Body of Christ results from the concord of charity. And as the Body of Christ is to the grains of wheat. so also is the blood to the grapes. For wine pours forth from the pressing, and what was individually in

How Do We Get There?

The preliminary gathering with catechesis can be an effective way eventually to introduce changes in the assembly's ritual behavior.

MYSTAGOGY

A second way of formation for the eucharistic prayer that is in the context of the liturgy itself is mystagogy, "an explanation of the mysteries celebrated." Here, the mystagogue expounds on the experience of

---

many grapes flows together into one liquid and becomes wine. Hence both in the bread and in the cup the sacrament of unity is present.

At the table of the Lord you hear the words, "The Lord be with you." We usually say these words when we greet you from the apse, and also whenever we begin prayers, because our well-being requires that the Lord be always with us, since without the Lord we are nothing. Recall, too, the words which sounded in your ears, the ones you say at the altar of God. For we question you, as it were, and admonish you, saying, "Lift up your hearts." Do not let them sink. The heart rots on earth, lift it towards heaven. But lift the heart to where? What do you answer? To where? "We have lifted them up to the Lord." Now to keep one's heart lifted up is sometimes a good thing and sometimes a bad thing. How can it be bad? It is bad for those of whom it was said: "You cast them down when they were lifted up" (Psalm 72:18). To lift up the heart, if not to the Lord, is not righteousness but arrogance. Therefore, when we say "Lift up your hearts," you answer, since to lift up the heart could be mere arrogance, "We have lifted them up to the Lord." And thus it becomes a worthy

deed, and not a mark of pride. But because it is a worthy act to lift up the heart to God, is that, then, a matter of our own doing? Could we accomplish this by our own power? Have we lifted up the earth which we are into heaven? Not at all! It is the Lord's doing, it is the Lord's condescension. The Lord stretched forth a hand, proffered grace, made upward that which was downward. Thus, when I said, "Lift up your hearts," and you made the reply, "We have lifted them up to the Lord," so you may not attribute to yourselves the lifting of your hearts, I added "Let us give thanks to the Lord our God."

These are concise mysteries, but vast ones. Our utterances are short, but full of meaning. For you say these things quickly, without the aid of a book, without reading, without the use of many words. Remember well what you are, and in whom you must persevere, so that you may be able to attain to the promises of God.

Augustine of Hippo. Excerpts from D. Sheerin, Eucharist, Message of the Fathers of the Church 7 *(Wilmington: Michael Glazier, 1986), pp. 100–102. © 1986 Michael Glazier Company. Used by permission of The Liturgical Press.*

eucharistic prayer with an eye to drawing out the meaning of the words or gestures experienced in light of the mystery of the pasch. The tone is not didactic but engages memory, symbol, allusion, metaphor and story to accomplish its task.[4] While the homily (especially during the paschal season) is envisioned as the most appropriate occasion for mystagogy, separate "mystagogical gatherings" immediately after the liturgy in the church might be offered. These might resemble the following:

- Opening refrain or song verse

A portion of a song just sung could provide an opening.

- Mystagogy

Then the mystagogue—who does not necessarily have to be the same person as the presider—would expound on the aspect of the celebration to be considered.

- Concluding prayer

A brief prayer would close the session.

- Blessing and Dismissal

Presider: May Christ, who opened the eyes of the blind to behold the presence of God and unstopped the ears of the deaf to hear the good news of salvation, strengthen you in faith and love.
All: Amen.

Homilists need to recall that not only are the scriptures the basis for the homily, but the liturgical texts of the day can be as well (GIRM, 41). While the homily then may not be a full-blown mystagogy, it can provide occasion for preaching on parts of the prefaces, the eucharistic prayers or even the acclamations themselves.[5]

MUSICAL PREPARATION

The music ministry of the parish has extra work to do. In addition to participating in the formation for prayer, the musicians need careful rehearsals of the music for the eucharistic prayer, and the cantors and directors of music need to spend much time with the presiders. The acclamations to the prayer and the singing of the prayer are not something to be decided 15 minutes before the liturgy.

The parish liturgical leadership needs to set out at the beginning of the liturgical cycle the course of eucharistic praying: which prayer in which season with which acclamations and how they will be done. Again, one set of acclamations might serve the parish for the whole cycle. New acclamations should be introduced with care that the assembly can learn them by heart and sing them with the aid of printed music or repeating after the cantor. The preliminary gathering might be the occasion to introduce the music in a context of prayer and give a chance to explain what acclamation is about.

If the director of music discerns that the presider is competent to sing the prayer, she or he might prepare a tape for the presider, schedule rehearsals during the week and help the presider memorize a melody and sustain a pitch. The first things to be worked on are the transitions from prayer to acclamation or from spoken text to sung text, so as to create a seamless garment.

NOTES

1. P. Rouillard, "From Human Meal to Christian Eucharist," in *Living Bread, Saving Cup: Readings on the Eucharist*, ed. R. K. Seasoltz (Collegeville: Liturgical Press, 1987), 129–130.

2. *Book of Blessings* (Collegeville: Liturgical Press, 1989), 13.

3. See NCCB Secretariat for the Liturgy, *In Spirit and Truth: Black Catholic Reflections on the Order of Mass* (Washington, D.C.: United States Catholic Conference, 1987), 9; and *Plenty Good Room: The Spirit and Truth of African American Catholic Worship* (Washington, D.C.: United States Catholic Conference, 1990), 112.

4. Those who wish to learn the art of mystagogy should first read the works of the great mystagogues themselves. See E. Yarnold, *The Awe-Inspiring Rites of Initiation*, 2d ed. (Collegeville: Liturgical Press, 1994), 67–250. For further help in crafting mystagogy on the eucharistic prayer, see the patristic texts collected by D. J. Sheerin, *The Eucharist*, Message of the Fathers of the Church 7 (Wilmington: Michael Glazier, 1986). See also the *Rite of Christian Initiation of Adults*, 244–247.

5. See Gabe Huck, *Preaching about the Mass* (Chicago: Liturgy Training Publications, 1992).

WHAT MIGHT THE FUTURE HOLD?

C an't no one know at sunrise
How this day is going to end.
Can't no one know at sunset
If the next day will begin.[1]

But we baptized flesh who live and move and have our being in this weary world do know that even if this day is our last, we must do what is ours to do—and we must do it well.

Charged by Jesus' command, we remember the mighty deeds God has done for us time and again, even when we least expected and in ways we never could have imagined.

We give thanks because we, like Miriam of old, have come dry-shod through the muck and, with hip bent and timbrel in hand, dance before the God who made us.

We call on God to send the Spirit and set afire our bread and wine, to tether us in love and to bring our dreams to reality. "Can't no one know" what might come, but we hope because we know that with our God, all things are possible.

And so on Sunday, the Lord's day, we gather. We take that without which human joy could not be sustained—food and drink, bread and wine—and we stand in awe. We lift up our hearts and lift up our arms in praise of this God. We show forth in our flesh what we are: the Body of Christ making our prayer before the throne of grace. We pray the eucharistic prayer.

As baptized daughters and sons of God, we must take seriously our vocation. We pray, listen, acclaim, offer, entreat, assent.

Bishops and presbyters are charged further with the awesome task of being the voice of the Body of Christ, making audible the yearnings of the hearts gathered before the altar-table. These are mighty words, as St. Basil said,[2] and they demand the very best that we can give them: our best voice, our best posture, our best music, our best attitude, our best gesture.

Striving for the realization of the eucharistic prayer as the most important prayer of the Sunday Mass, we call forth full, conscious and active participation of the faithful and full, conscious and active presiding. Yet we realize that both must engage the lavish use of symbol, the reverencing of rhythm and ritual, the crafting and deployment of space and the attention to detail.

Our eucharistic praying must mine memories in images of a pregnant virgin, satiated crowds, scandalous suppers, anointed feet, broken bread and an empty tomb. We must gather and tell the stories that make up those memories. And we must continue to empty ourselves — sacrifice ourselves — in the words of praise and thanksgiving and in our life lived in service to the poor, the battered down and the scorned.

For this is what has largely eluded us so far in the liturgical renewal: For us baptized people, words of doxology shape and transform our life, our world, our bread and wine, our history. Our hope cuts through the present pain, and our action for justice and fellowship of love are inseparable from our eucharist. Convinced that God hears the cry the poor, we can hope for the glory that will be ours when "all shall be well and / All manner of thing shall be well."[3]

Yet, as we await with hope, we acknowledge that much is still not well. The number of parishes that want for a presbyter to draw together their thanksgiving and praise and voice the eucharistic prayer is growing at an alarming rate. In a time when Christians of many denominations take up the same words of eucharist, the Body of Christ is still sundered. The common pattern of eucharistic praying should be the source of our unity, the call to a common table.

At that table, we will join our voices with every creature under heaven and proclaim:

> It is fitting and right, just and right, here and everywhere to give you thanks, Lord, holy Father, eternal God: You snatched us from perpetual death and the last darkness of hell, and gave mortal matter, put together from the liquid mud, to your Son and to eternity. Who is acceptable to tell your praises, who can make a full declaration of your works? Every tongue marvels at you![4]

NOTES

1. Ysaye Maria Barnwell, "Spiritual," on *Still on the Journey*, Sweet Honey in the Rock, EarthBeat! Records (Redway, Calif.), CD 9 42536-2.

2. Basil the Great, *Peri tou agiou pneumatos* (27:66), in Trait'é du Saint-Esprit, ed. B. Pruch' (Angers, 1947), 234, # 55a.

3. Thomas Stearns Eliot, "Little Gidding" in *T.S. Eliot: Collected Poems 1909–1962* (San Diego, Harcourt Brace Jovanovich, 1963), 209.

4. The *contestatio* of a Gallican eucharistic prayer for Sunday, in R. C. D. Jasper and G. J. Cuming, *Prayers of the Eucharist: Early and Reformed* (New York: Pueblo, 1987), 148.

The Eucharistic Prayer Is an Act of the Whole Assembly

The following is taken from a talk given by Joseph Gelineau, SJ, at the Universa Laus meeting in 1994. The full text appeared in the February 1997 issue of Pastoral Music *magazine.*

Must we not overcome a serious deficiency — the present-day passivity of too many assemblies during the eucharistic prayer?

Acclamations

We can say that in the workings of the Consilium group, given the task of reforming the Mass after Vatican II, the image of the eucharistic prayer as a continuous discourse (along the lines of Antiochene models of the eucharistic prayer) predominated. All the Consilium members were acquainted with Eastern church usages in which not only the priest had a part in the eucharistic action, but also the deacon, the choir, and the people. Furthermore, when it came time to consider appropriate forms of active participation, the notion of singing immediately came to the fore. Thus there is no reason to be surprised that the suggestion was made to introduce into the eucharistic prayer acclamations for the assembly — without any prejudice to the acclamatory elements that were already part of this prayer in the Roman Rite: the preface dialogue, the Sanctus, and the final Amen.

After discussion of various possibilities, the memorial acclamation was retained as a new acclamation to be proposed. It was linked to the words *mysterium fidei*, taken from the *verba Domini* of the institution account.[1] Other acclamations were proposed. But this was asking too much, and we had to be content with proposing the four sung interventions that are now familiar to us (preface dialogue, Sanctus, memorial acclamation, Amen).

As expected, pastors concerned about the assembly's active participation were not long in observing that, in many cases, the four sung moments were not sufficient to retain the assembly's attention. When the eucharistic prayers for Masses with children were prepared, a certain extension of the number of acclamations was accepted.

With this as our starting point, we have experienced, both in large eucharistic assemblies and in certain festive liturgies, the development of various types of acclamations added to the original four: acclamations of praise throughout the preface, of supplication in the intercessions, of adoration at each consecration, and of petition at the two epicleses (invocations of the Spirit).

In spite of a rather strong movement toward the use of additional acclamations, the realization of such developments remain limited. Even in using the eucharistic prayers for Masses with children, certain priests have suppressed use of the acclamations provided, precisely, they say, in order to promote the active participation of the children! In any case, the parish Sunday eucharist has not seen any decisive and lasting progress in this direction.

A survey of the effectiveness of acclamations as a way of assembly participation in the eucharistic action reveals advantages as well as disadvantages.

ADVANTAGES If the acclamation is short, quite powerful, and easily memorized, this is the simplest way of having the assembly actively participate in the eucharistic prayer. In addition, this model is suitable for assemblies of any size and of diverse cultural levels.

DISADVANTAGES Its ease of use is also an acclamation's weakness. A pure and simple repetition quickly wearies. This can already be true when an acclamation is repeated within the same celebration. It is even more of a danger Sunday after Sunday during the year. In addition, the current acclamations found in all the eucharistic prayers are, broadly speaking, specific to their place and composed of coherent unities, even though there are three texts for the assembly in the preface dialogue, four texts in the Sanctus, and three in each of the memorial acclamations. Even the doublet of the Hosanna, which might be an avenue for adaptation, cannot, since the recurrence of "Hosanna in the highest" leads to the priest's reprise: *Vere Sanctus* ("Lord, you are holy indeed"). Compositions where this cry is repeated to satiety become tiresome and heavy. Additionally, a short, repeated acclamation is popular only in certain cultures or in liturgical forms that are naturally responsorial, like the litany. In our Western world popular melodies often need to be stretched out.

The greatest drawback of "added" acclamations is that rather than moving the prayer onward, they put a brake on it by constantly cutting up the basic discourse and halting its progress. Even the insertion of the memorial acclamation in the official eucharistic prayers does not avoid this weakness — though it has been remedied in the eucharistic prayers for Masses with children where the people's memorial echoes that of the priest.

One acceptable way of adding acclamations would be to develop a dialogue form such as we find, for example, in the Coptic liturgy. There the single institution narrative contains 17 acclamatory interventions, but each is linked to the words that precede it. In conclusion, the acclamation, if it is going to be a good vehicle for participation, should be intelligently used and cast within the globality of the speech and the action.

Diversified Globality

I began with the elements of the missal of Paul VI in their order and according to their nature. And so it was that I rediscovered something that would become very valuable to me. I discovered that eucharistic action is an ensemble composed of differentiated parts whose unity should nonetheless remain evident.

But first of all I had to ask the question, when does the eucharistic prayer truly begin? I belong to the generation of liturgists who, some thirty years ago in the beautiful days of the "dialogue" Mass with the first French chants for the Mass, knew an over-valuation of the offertory, which provoked a counter-current by enlightened spirits. This can partially explain

why Coetus X of the Consilium, having suppressed the former offertory prayers, treated this ritual moment (renamed the "preparation of the gifts") in a minor mode, especially in regard to singing. And yet the people were given the double response "Blessed be God for ever"; and Pope Paul VI requested that the *Orate, fratres* with its response be retained. Consequently the whole rite has little coherence. Rather than making this rite a true opening of the eucharist, we often wind up with some sort of dead time, furnished with the prayers that the priest says aloud (which was not anticipated) and the recited responses of the assembly.

Before the Second Vatican Council, I had adapted the offertory rite by using various chants for what I conceived this rite to be: the beginning of the eucharist. An especially successful chant was a processional piece with the assembly's refrain "You alone are holy," inspired by the great entrance of the Liturgy of St. John Chrysostom.[2] After the introduction of the eucharistic prayers proclaimed aloud and in the vernacular, I discovered that each time this chant was sung, it provided a special "relief" to the presider's words as he began the eucharistic prayer — the chant made the prayer easier to hear and made it seem shorter. And so I came to realize that it was necessary to place a *high* value on this first moment, which I call the "opening of the eucharist."

This realization is the first landmark of what I am here calling "diversified globality." The eucharistic prayer, the *anaphora* (to use that beautiful word adorned with rich images, a word taken from our Greek brothers and sisters), ascends and is raised from the meal table on which we have just placed the gifts, and it will return there for the breaking of the bread. The first moment of this global experience thus consists of a procession throughout the whole assembly — which is also a priming of the pump for the going-and-returning of the mysterious eucharistic exchange — accompanied by singing which already places the participants in an act of praise. Everything begins here.

Then the presider can initiate the praise by means of the dialogue; he can cantillate the preface, the public testimony of the *mirabilia Dei*, leading the assembly, in union with the angels, to the hymn of the seraphim: Sanctus, Sanctus, Sanctus.

Using the official melodies for the dialogue and the preface poses no problem. But there should be a link — not only in terms of meaning but a living and musical link — between the end of the preface and the beginning of the Sanctus. It was especially necessary in the postconciliar reform to regain the specific character of the acclamatory nature of the Sanctus, which is too often treated as a *lied*. In fact the Sanctus is a threefold alternating adoration: "Holy, holy, holy"; the first proclamation — Heaven and earth are full . . ."; the acclamation "Hosanna in the highest"; the second proclamation: "Blessed is he who comes . . ."; and finally the repetition of the "Hosanna in the highest," but introducing the *Vere sanctus* of the presider. *Sanctus XVIII* in the *Kyriale* gives us a wonderful example of how this works.

The institution narrative block of the prayer was once more enriched by the cantillation of the *verba Domini*, followed respectively by the two worshiping "Amens" of the whole assembly [not used in current North American practice] inspired by the liturgies of the East but very well received by the piety of the faithful of the West.

French assemblies quickly adopted the singing of the memorial acclamation, and its practice was fruitful.

There remained the final Amen, evidently too weak to function as a crown for the whole prayer. We tried to use more extended "Amens" or multiple or glossed Amens, or Amens interpolated within the *Per ipsum*. But none of this appeared convincing.

As to the fundamental question I have posed here — the ritual distance between an extensive presidential word and an evidently weak participation of the assembly in the *sacrificium laudis* — I could find no solution.

It was at the conclusion of this stage of a double investigation, one on the proper shape of each participatory moment and the other on the globality experienced in a unified and continuous action, that I left Paris to become the parish priest of five small parishes south of the Fontainbleu forest.

The Integral Action

In my five parishes the assemblies were small in number and rather poor in resources of all kinds, but very open to common prayer, which was sung and already communitarian thanks to Sunday assemblies that for many years were conducted by the laity of the place two Sundays a month. To develop a eucharist which would be the action of the whole assembly remained my permanent concern. But I knew that such an experience was not present most of the time.

It seemed to me that the only certain way of attaining this was through *auto*-inculturation, namely, by an investigation involving the participants themselves, in light of God's word and the church's tradition, in light of a living and expressive celebration, interior and prayerful. I adopted the seven points of #55 of the *General Instruction of the Roman Missal*, the texts given in the official books, the existing chants. My goal was to have a successful ritual montage.

I began by selecting, among the 200 musical settings of the French text for the Sanctus, one with a chance of being sung well by all, of sufficiently expressing the meaning of this moment of praise, and, especially, of being able to endure long use. I opted for a music having bonds with Breton folklore.[3] Fifteen years later, we still sing it almost every Sunday.

The dialogue before the preface quickly became a special moment of song when the voices of all, especially those of the children, sound loud and clear, because this is an invariable moment, which is ritually well assimilated.

The preface is usually cantillated, and in such a way that it can be uninterruptedly joined to the intonation by all of the Sanctus, most often sung without accompaniment, which gives value to the voice of God's people as such.

The *verba Domini* of the institution narrative are always cantillated in order to situate these words, cited and re-cited, on their foundational level. Each of the two citations leads to confession-adoration. In the beginning I used a double Amen, rather simple yet without much depth, till the day when I tried the responses composed by Didier Rimaud and Jacques Berthier for a Mass at the time of a papal trip[4]:

"Body of Christ, handed over for us!" "Blood of Christ, poured out for us!" On various occasions I have observed the excellent effect of these acclamations, classic and simple. Their reception was immediate and without regret.

For the memorial acclamation, we use one of the melodies universally received in France: "Gloire à toi qui étais mort."[5]

Of all the attempts undertaken to give fullness to the final Amen, none seems plausible to me. And so I adopted the doxology from Eucharistic Prayer I for Masses with Children, authorized in the French-language version, and which is satisfactory.[6]

Finally, and not without hesitation (but struck by the impact of this practice in various French assemblies both large and small) I introduced the double invocation of the Holy Spirit[7] where the people are associated to the two epicleses, the first over the gifts — "Let your Spirit come upon these gifts . . ." — and the second upon those who will receive the eucharist — "Grant that we . . . may be filled with his Holy Spirit, and become . . ." The first epiclesis is always very "pregnant." But the second is less so, undoubtedly because it uses the same music as the first epiclesis and, therefore, creates a sense of regression rather than a progression toward the communion.

I thus find myself with twelve musical pieces sung by the assembly; all are well received by its members, and yet they are successive and not unified. Is it not my role as a liturgist, as a composer, and as a celebrant, to link them together in a continuous and progressive whole, with direction and rhythm? The key to linking them was given to me by the technique of *ekphonesis*: In concluding a prayer or one section of a longer prayer, the minister raises the voice and "cantillates" the prayer's last words in such a way that the choir or assembly can immediately link its response to them. This is, in the best sense of the word, a collage — the kind of tinkering that a craft worker has to do in order to create a true work of art.

Ten years of such inculturation have resulted in a eucharistic action with a unified sense of flow in which the assembly is kept going by its sustained participation, with the highs and lows of waves giving rhythm to this action in a living manner.

Three Points for Further Attention

In reflecting on this experience, I believe it useful to mention three points that, in my mind, merit further attention: the fixity-flexibility relationship; the laws of oral public communication; and the importance of gesture and posture.

FIXITY AND FLEXIBILITY The success of the operative model, as explained above, is obviously connected with its ritualization. To ensure this model's success, its structure should be invariable. The rite, if it is to be taken up and interiorized by the assembly, must be incorporated by the assembly. The very fixity of the rite provides an opportunity for the free and unlimited creation of meaning.

Nonetheless, the absolute fixity of the whole text of the eucharistic prayer is not necessarily the best means of sustaining the attention of the assembly. In a fixed framework there must be variable parts calling for attention. It might be a different melody for the Sanctus or the anamnesis. It might be a variable part of the text as we find in the new eucharistic prayers. I have discovered great pastoral benefit by modulating the more flexible moments of the eucharistic prayer, within the *Vere Sanctus*, in the circumstances of the institution narrative, in diverse intercessions. This helps revitalize the significant major invariants that bind together the whole action.

LAWS OF PUBLIC ORAL COMMUNICATION Previous to Vatican II, the liturgy was based on what was written down. Everything came from a book and was recited in a dead language. The reform of the rites necessarily requires the art of public oral communication. The reformers were caught short by this, since public oral communication is a very rare art today. Even the modern media call for modes of communication that are not those of the liturgical assembly: They are addressed to individuals and not to a gathered people. And so we must regain the techniques presumed by the liturgy. Without being able to develop at length this very important point for the eucharistic prayer, allow me to recall several principles. Public oral communication presumes:

■ the transmission of a message by means of a living word and not by simply reading a book (the obvious exception is the Bible);

■ a determined and invariable order of successive episodes that comprise the whole account;

■ standard formulas for beginning each new episode;

■ a certain flexibility to expand or shorten certain passages as it proves useful;

- the untouchable character of certain formulas in regard to symbolic and sacred value;

- if the hearers intervene, there must be coded moments for this.

We can easily apply these rules to the eucharistic prayer.

POSTURE AND GESTURE, WORDS AND CHANTS

Finally, I would like to emphasize what I believe is becoming increasingly important in the celebration of the eucharistic prayer: The connection between what is done by means of gestures and what is said through words, whether these words are cantillated or sung, must be perceptible.

If the Sanctus is a musical piece rendered for its own sake, with no link to what precedes and what follows it, its music, no matter what type, will quickly wear out, and we will have to change it often. If the Sanctus is a collective action integrated into a ritual whole and is intimately united to this whole, we can employ the same melody without fear of rapid erosion.

If the epiclesis invocation accompanies a slow and downward gesture of the celebrant or celebrants, words and melodies are part of the action and can no longer be separated from it. Thus the words of reverence "Body of Christ" or "Amen" are sung while the presider is still holding up the bread or the cup.

If the eucharistic action begins with a great processional chant—the "song of the mysteries"—during which the bread and wine are brought to the altar, and if the action concludes with the division of the holy gifts in a litany or a *confractorium* antiphon, each of the symbolic elements — gestures, postures, words and singing—will reinforce each other.

Must we recall that it should not be the presider alone at the altar who is facing all, but he is to be surrounded by ministers or by the faithful, since the presider first of all acts *in persona ecclesiae*? When eyes are riveted upon a book, a prayer of praise addressed to God in the name of the whole assembled people is difficult to sustain. The presider's tones of voice should not be those of his own individual person but those of the church at prayer. In my view, all this is part of an integrated celebration and constitutes its evident conditions.

A very precious treasure has been entrusted to us, but it largely remains to be inculturated so that it can be celebrated in assemblies of all nations in a living manner, one that is meaningful and efficacious of the action of the Spirit.

NOTES

1. As in certain Eastern Church models, this acclamation is addressed to Christ. And this choice of address is related to the observations of J. A. Jungmann on the people's prayer as being intentionally addressed to Christ and taking the place of the priest's prayer which is addressed to the Father.

2. Fiche C54, T. and M. P. M. Hoog, ed. Chalet.

3. "Saint" E. Daniel – A 176, ed. Fleurus.

4. Messe "Vienne la paix" T. D. Rimaud-M. J. Berthier, ed. S. M.

5. Fiche CL 5-3, ed. S. M.

6. "Gloire à toi, Père très bon" VL 5–3, ed. S. M.

7. Music extracted from "Saint" C 178 of J. Berthier, ed. Fleurus.

Excerpts from Joseph Gelineau, SJ, "Making the Eucharistic Prayer an Act of the Whole Assembly," in Pastoral Music, *vol. 21:3 (February-March 1997). Copyright © 1997 by the National Association of Pastoral Musicians. Used with permission.*

BULLETIN INSERTS

he materials on the following pages may be reproduced by purchasers of this book for use in parishes and other institutions. The proper acknowledgment should appear whenever these pages are duplicated.

The Eucharistic Prayer

WHAT IS THE EUCHARISTIC PRAYER? It is the prayer the church makes from the time we "lift up our hearts" until we sing the great Amen before the Our Father.

The *General Instruction of the Roman Missal* states: "The center and summit of the entire celebration begins: the eucharistic prayer, a prayer of thanksgiving and sanctification. . . . The entire congregation joins itself to Christ in acknowledging the great things God has done."

The priest doesn't do it alone! We, the assembled church, do this eucharistic praying together!

We come around the altar bearing gifts of bread and wine and ourselves. In the eucharistic prayer we give thanks and praise. We remember the mighty deeds God has done for us through Christ Jesus in the Holy Spirit. We surrender ourselves in praise. Our memory of God's steadfast love for us culminates in the memory of the pasch of Jesus, his passion, death, resurrection and mission of the Spirit.

Jesus commanded, "Do this in remembrance of me." And in the eucharistic prayer, we say, "Therefore, Lord, we do remember." Remembering, we call upon God to send the Holy Spirit over our gifts and over us that we the church may be transformed through our sharing in the Body and Blood of Christ.

With the Spirit's help we pray to God to remember the church, the saints and our beloved dead. We plead with God to continue to be in our midst in a communion pledged and shared in the Body and Blood of Christ. Our thanksgiving, remembrance and supplication swell to the concluding praise of God through Jesus Christ.

The eucharistic prayer is indeed the prayer of the whole assembly. But we are an "ordered" assembly. Thus, while the whole assembly celebrates and prays the eucharistic prayer, one member of the body gives it voice because he is the presider of the assembly, called and ordered by the bishop. The praying of the eucharistic prayer is the work of all the baptized; the voicing of the prayer is the work of the ordained minister. As the fifth-century bishop Theodore of Mopsuestia said, the presider is the "common tongue of the body."

The eucharistic prayer is more than words on a page: It a way of praying. It is a way of living. Praying the eucharistic prayer at Sunday Mass requires much of us. It means that we must come to do our prayer having struggled to live lives of thanksgiving day in and day out. We, the baptized, members of the Body of Christ, live out our baptismal calling by our eucharistic prayer.

La Plegaria Eucarística

¿QUÉ ES LA PLEGARIA EUCARÍSTICA? Es la oración que la Iglesia hace desde el momento en que "levantamos nuestros corazones" hasta el gran Amén antes del Padre nuestro.

La *Instrucción General para el Uso del Misal Romano* declara: "Es el punto central y el momento culminante de toda la celebración; es una plegaria de acción de gracias y santificación. . . . La congregación de los fieles se une con Cristo en el reconocimiento de las grandezas de Dios".

¡El sacerdote no lo hace solo! ¡Nosotros, la asamblea reunida, hacemos esta Plegaria Eucarística!

Nos acercamos al altar trayendo el pan y el vino y a nosotros mismos. En ella alabamos y damos gracias a Dios. Recordamos la acción poderosa que Dios ha hecho para nosotros a través de Cristo Jesús en el Espíritu Santo. Nos rendimos así en oración profunda. Nuestra memoria del amor constante que Dios ha tenido por nosotros culmina en la memoria de la Pascua de Jesús.

Jesús mandó, "Hagan esto en memoria mía". Y en la Plegaria Eucarística nosotros decimos, "por lo tanto, nosotros lo hacemos Señor". Haciéndolo, pedimos a Dios que mande el Espíritu Santo sobre nuestros dones y sobre los que formamos la Iglesia.

Con la ayuda del Espíritu oramos a Dios para que recuerde a la Iglesia, los santos, y nuestros amados difuntos. Suplicamos a Dios que continúe en medio de nosotros. Nuestra acción de gracias, nuestra memoria y nuestras súplicas, se hacen más grandes al concluir nuestra oración a Dios a través de Jesucristo.

La Plegaria Eucarística es verdaderamente la oración de la asamblea entera. Pero nosotros somos una asamblea "ordenada". Así, mientras la asamblea entera celebra y proclama la Plegaria Eucarística, un miembro de la asamblea da su voz. El, llamado y ordenado por el Obispo, es quien la preside. La proclamación de la Plegaria Eucarística es trabajo de todos los bautizados; la recitación de la Plegaria en la asamblea es el trabajo de un ministro ordenado. Como lo dijo el Obispo del Siglo V Theodore de Mopsuestia, la "lengua común del cuerpo".

La Plegaria Eucarística es más que unas palabras escritas en una página: es una manera de vivir. Proclamar la Plegaria Eucarística en la Misa dominical significa que nosotros debemos venir a hacer nuestra oración luchando por vivir nuestra vida en continua acción de gracias viviendo así nuestro llamado bautismal.

Posture

A PRIMARY WAY in which the assembly takes part in the praying of the eucharistic prayer is by posture. Our posture gives visible expression of our interior lives of thanksgiving and praise and to our understanding of the eucharistic celebration.

Standing was the ancient posture of the whole assembly at the eucharistic prayer. Times and pieties changed, and kneeling became the posture of the assembly in the West, while the presider stood. Now, in our effort to recover the meaning of the eucharistic prayer as the whole assembly's prayer of thanksgiving, standing — which remained the assembly's posture at the eucharistic prayer in many parts of Christianity — has again been suggested as the posture for all to assume.

■ **We stand victorious.** We stand as those who, having been baptized into Christ's death, rise "to walk in newness of life" (Romans 6:4). We who share in Christ's victory over death stand to give thanks and praise to God, who pours forth the Spirit to make us one.

■ **We stand obedient.** In our eucharistic prayer we recall the Lord's command, "Do this is memory of me." And we obey, remembering Christ's saving deeds in our prayer over bread and wine.

■ **We stand in awe.** We enter into the song of the heavenly hosts and stand before God crying Holy! We stand and marvel at all our God has done for us and welcome the Spirit. We draw near to the Lord Jesus. We stand with attention, eager to draw near the table of Christ's body and blood.

■ **We stand ready.** We stand ready to go forth from our assembly into the world to be broken and poured out in service to all.

We are a pilgrim people and know that we have no lasting place here. We stand ready to greet the Lord, who will come again, and we stand ready to march to the banquet of heaven. We do not stand any which way. We stand up straight, attentively.

■ All could assume the ancient prayer position, known as the "praying," or *orans*, position: hands uplifted to the height of one's head with the palms facing outward and slightly upward. Our uplifted hands embody our thanksgiving and supplication: We lift up our hearts, lift up our praise, lift up our thanksgiving as we lift up our hands. With arms outstretched we offer ourselves as a living sacrifice of praise and bear witness to the passion of Christ on the cross with our bodies.

■ Or we could keep our hands folded, lifted up and held at our heart. In this way we remain conscious of our praying and show forth with our body our prayer of thanks and praise.

Postura

LA PRIMERA FORMA en que la asamblea toma parte en la oración de la Plegaria Eucarística es a través de la postura. Esta es una expresión visible del interior de nuestras vidas, de nuestra alabanza y acción de gracias, y de nuestro entendimiento de la celebración Eucarística.

Estar de pie durante la Plegaria Eucarística, es una postura ancestral de toda la asamblea. Sin embargo, han cambiado los tiempos y las piedades, y el arrodillarse se convirtió en una postura de la asamblea del Oeste, mientras el que preside permanece de pie. En nuestro esfuerzo por recobrar el sentido de la Plegaria Eucarística como la acción de gracias de la asamblea entera, levantarse se quedó como la postura oficial de la asamblea en el momento de la Plegaria Eucarística en muchas otras partes de la Cristiandad.

■ **De pie, permanecemos victoriosos.** Como aquellos que, habiendo sido bautizados en la muerte de Cristo, resucitan "para caminar en una vida nueva" (Romans 6:4). Los que compartimos la victoria de Cristo sobre la muerte, nos ponemos de pie para continuar alabando a Dios, quien ha derramado su Espíritu sobre nosotros a fin de que seamos uno.

■ **De pie, permanecemos obedientes.** En nuestra Plegaria Eucarística recordamos el mandato del Señor, "Hagan esto en memoria mía". Y obedecemos al Señor, recordando la acción salvífica de Cristo en nuestra oración sobre el pan y el vino.

■ **De pie, permanecemos en asombro.** Entramos a formar parte del coro celestial y de pie, ante Dios, aclamamos ¡Santo! De pie, continuamos maravillados por todo lo que Dios ha hecho por nosotros y recibimos al Espíritu Santo. Nos acercamos al Señor Jesús. Permanecemos de pie, atentos, con un deseo ardiente de acercarnos al altar del Cuerpo y la Sangre de Cristo.

■ **De pie, permanecemos listos.** Estamos listos para ir hacia el mundo, para estar al servicio de los demás. Sabemos que no tenemos una permanencia eterna aquí en la tierra. Por lo tanto, nos mantenemos listos para saludar al Señor quien vendrá de nuevo y a la vez estamos listos para participar del banquete celestial.

■ Todos pueden asumir la antigua posición, conocida como la "orante" o posición del orante: las manos levantadas a la altura de la cabeza, y las palmas hacia arriba. Las manos levantadas encarnan nuestra súplica y acción de gracias: levantamos nuestros corazones, elevamos nuestra alabanza, nuestra acción de gracias al mismo tiempo que levantamos nuestras manos. Nos ofrecemos nosotros mismos como un sacrificio viviente de oración.

Acclamations

WE, THE CHURCH, pray the eucharistic prayer by our acclamations:

- the Holy, Holy, Holy
- the Memorial Acclamation
- the Great Amen

When we sing the Holy, Holy, Holy, we join our voices to the choirs of the angels and all the hosts of heaven. Singing praise and thanksgiving, we are lifted up through Christ. We join in the eternal prayer of Christ to the Father in the Spirit of love. In our eucharistic prayer, earth is joined to heaven. All things seen and unseen — all reality — are caught up in thanksgiving.

The acclamation that we sing after the Last Supper account acclaims Jesus, whose memorial command we keep. Our singing of the memorial acclamation manifests our participation in the memorial thanksgiving and expresses our obedience to Christ's command. When we sing "Christ has died, Christ is risen, Christ will come again," or "Dying you destroyed our death," this is not an interruption in the prayer. It *is* the prayer. We proclaim the paschal joy of life in the risen Christ, who will come again in glory.

Amen means "What you have said is true" and "So be what you have said." Amen, the original acclamation of the eucharistic prayer, is our assent to what the presider voices as the prayer of the church, our prayer. When we ring out with the great Amen, we are saying that indeed this prayer is the prayer of the church here gathered.

We sing these acclamations. Music embodies thanksgiving the way posture does. Singing the acclamations unites us in a common breathing that shows forth the unity of our action: joining with the choirs of heaven, proclaiming the mystery of faith, and assenting to the whole prayer. Music engages our bodies in a way that simple speech cannot. To sing shifts our posture and shakes our created frame.

Singing engages muscle, breath, heart and soul. It wells up from our core, moves us to joy and tears. We, the Spirit-filled Body of Christ, as best we can, sing forth by the power of the Spirit, who can turn even the flattest groans into glorias.

Aclamaciones

LA IGLESIA ORA con la Plegaria Eucarística a través de nuestras aclamaciones:

- El Santo, Santo, Santo
- la Aclamación memorial
- el gran Amén

Cuando cantamos el Santo, Santo, Santo, acompañamos las voces de los coros de ángeles y todos aquellos que están en el cielo. Cantando la alabanza y la acción de gracias, somos elevados por Cristo. Somos parte de la oración eterna de Cristo al Padre en el Espíritu de amor. En nuestra oración eucarística, la tierra se une con el cielo. Todas las cosas visibles e invisibles —todas realmente— son acogidas en nuestra acción de gracias.

La aclamación que cantamos después de la narración de la Ultima Cena aclama a Jesús, de quien cumplimos este mandato. Nuestro canto de la aclamación memorial manifiesta nuestra participación en la acción de gracias y expresa nuestra obediencia al mandato de Cristo. Cuando cantamos "Cristo ha muerto, Cristo ha resucitado, Cristo vendrá de nuevo", o "Muriendo destruyó nuestra muerte", no es una interrupción de la oración. *Es* la oración. Nosotros proclamamos el gozo pascual de la vida en Cristo resucitado, quien vendrá de nuevo lleno de gloria.

Amén significa: "Así sea". "Lo que has dicho es cierto" y "sea como Tú lo has dicho". Amén, la aclamación original de la Plegaria Eucarística, es nuestro asentimiento a la voz de quienes presiden la oración de la Iglesia, nuestra oración. Cuando resonamos con el gran Amén, estamos diciendo verdaderamente que esta oración es la oración de la Iglesia reunida.

Cantamos estas aclamaciones. La música se incorpora a la acción de gracias en la misma manera que lo hace la postura. Cantando las aclamaciones comunes, nos unimos en un aliento común que va siempre adelante y que manifiesta la unidad de nuestra acción: acompañando a los coros del cielo, proclamando el misterio de nuestra fe y afirmando con la Plegaria entera. La música envuelve nuestros cuerpos en una manera en que simplemente el discurso no lo puede hacer. Al cantar lo hacemos con gran entusiasmo, de tal manera que incluya todo nuestro ser.

Cantando se incorporan los músculos, aliento, el alma y el corazón. Se eleva desde nuestro corazón, para luego desbordar en alegría. Nosotros, el Cuerpo de Cristo, lleno del Espíritu Santo, de la mejor. manera que podamos hacerlo, continuamos cantando por la fuerza del mismo Espíritu, quien puede tornar nuestros gemidos en verdaderas alabanzas.